September–December 2022

Edited by **Rachel Tranter** and **Olivia Warburton**

15 The Chambers, Vineyard
Abingdon OX14 3FE
brf.org.uk

Bible Reading Fellowship is a charity (233280)
and company limited by guarantee (301324),
registered in England and Wales

ISBN 978 1 80039 134 5
All rights reserved

This edition © Bible Reading Fellowship 2022
Cover image © agsandrew/stock.adobe.com

Distributed in Australia by:
MediaCom Education Inc, PO Box 610, Unley, SA 5061
Tel: 1 800 811 311 | admin@mediacom.org.au

Distributed in New Zealand by:
Scripture Union Wholesale, PO Box 760, Wellington
Tel: 04 385 0421 | suwholesale@clear.net.nz

Acknowledgements

Scripture quotations marked with the following acronyms are taken from the
version shown. Where no acronym is given, the quotation is taken from the
version stated in the contributor's introduction. ESV: The Holy Bible, English
Standard Version, published by HarperCollins Publishers, © 2001 Crossway Bibles,
a division of Good News Publishers. Used by permission. All rights reserved. NASB:
The New American Standard Bible®, Copyright © by The Lockman Foundation.
Used by permission. NIV: The Holy Bible, New International Version (Anglicised
edition) copyright © 1979, 1984, 2011 by Biblica. Used by permission of Hodder
& Stoughton Publishers, a Hachette UK company. All rights reserved. 'NIV' is a
registered trademark of Biblica. UK trademark number 1448790. NRSV: The New
Revised Standard Version of the Bible, Anglicised edition, copyright © 1989, 1995 by
the Division of Christian Education of the National Council of the Churches of Christ
in the United States of America. Used by permission. All rights reserved. RNJB: The
Revised New Jerusalem Bible © 2018, 2019 by Darton, Longman & Todd Ltd.

Every effort has been made to trace and contact copyright owners for material used
in this resource. We apologise for any inadvertent omissions or errors, and would
ask those concerned to contact us so that full acknowledgement can be made in
the future.

A catalogue record for this book is available from the British Library

Printed by Gutenberg Press, Tarxien, Malta

Suggestions for using *Guidelines*

Set aside a regular time and place, if possible, when and where you can read and pray undisturbed. Before you begin, take time to be still and, if you find it helpful, use the BRF centenary prayer on page 6.

In *Guidelines*, the introductory section provides context for the passages or themes to be studied, while the units of comment can be used daily, weekly or whatever best fits your timetable. You will need a Bible (more than one if you want to compare different translations), as Bible passages are not included. Please don't be tempted to skip the Bible reading because you know the passage well. We will have utterly failed if we don't bring our readers into engagement with the word of God. At the end of each week is a 'Guidelines' section, offering further thoughts about or practical application of what you have been studying.

Occasionally, you may read something in *Guidelines* that you find particularly challenging, even uncomfortable. This is inevitable in a series of notes which draws on a wide spectrum of contributors and doesn't believe in ducking difficult issues. Indeed, we believe that *Guidelines* readers much prefer thought-provoking material to a bland diet that only confirms what they already think.

If you do disagree with a contributor, you may find it helpful to go through these three steps. First, think about why you feel uncomfortable. Perhaps this is an idea that is new to you, or you are not happy about the way something has been expressed. Or there may be something more substantial – you may feel that the writer is guilty of sweeping generalisation, factual error or theological or ethical misjudgement. Second, pray that God would use this disagreement to teach you more about his word and about yourself. Third, have a deeper read about the issue. There are further reading suggestions at the end of each writer's block of notes. And then, do feel free to write to the contributor or the editor of *Guidelines*. We welcome communication, by email, phone or letter, as it enables us to discover what has been useful, challenging or infuriating for our readers. We don't always promise to change things, but we will always listen and think about your ideas, complaints or suggestions. Thank you!

To send feedback, please email **enquiries@brf.org.uk**, phone **+44 (0)1865 319700** or write to the address shown opposite.

Writers in this issue

Ashley Hibbard is a research associate at the Centre for the Study of Bible and Violence and an adjunct lecturer at African Christian College, Eswatini, and at Emmanuel Bible College, Kitchener, Canada.

Stephen Finamore is principal of Bristol Baptist College. Steve has worked as a pastor, a lawyer and in community development in inner London and the Peruvian Andes.

Ruth M. Bancewicz is church engagement director at The Faraday Institute for Science and Religion, Cambridge, where the other contributors to her notes are, or have been, also based.

Rosalee Velloso Ewell is a theologian from São Paulo, Brazil. She is director of church relations for the United Bible Societies and former principal of Redcliffe College. Rosalee lives with her family in Birmingham, UK.

Steve Walton is associate research fellow and part-time tutor in New Testament at Trinity College, Bristol. He is a retired international volleyball referee and lives in west London with his wife Ali, a vicar, and their Border Terrier, Flora.

Peter Hatton is a former tutor at Bristol Baptist College, where he taught after 25 years in Methodist pastoral ministry. Preaching, some writing projects and looking after grandchildren are keeping him occupied in 'retirement'.

David Spriggs is a Baptist minister who worked for the Evangelical Alliance and Bible Society. His interests are engaging people with the Bible, Christian leadership and prayer. He is now minister of a church in Leicester.

Henry Wansbrough is a monk of Ampleforth in Yorkshire. In his long career of teaching he has been chairman of the Oxford Faculty of Theology and has served on the Pope's Biblical Commission and on the Anglican Roman Catholic International Commission.

Matthew Knell has lectured in historical theology and church history at the London School of Theology for twelve years, covering Christian thought from the Church Fathers to the modern day.

Imogen Ball is a curate at All Saints, Trull, and St Michael's, Angersleigh. Her MA at Trinity College Bristol focused on women's studies in the Old Testament, specifically the womb.

Kate Bruce is an RAF Chaplain. Her PhD was in preaching and imagination, published as *Igniting the Heart* (SPCK, 2015). She regularly offers day conferences in preaching, and leads retreats.

The editors write...

Welcome to this issue of *Guidelines*! This is our first issue as editors, though we have been involved with *Guidelines* for a number of years, through our roles at BRF as Head of Content Creation (Olivia) and Editorial Manager (Rachel). We are grateful to Helen Paynter for her time as editor, which saw a number of new writers from different traditions join the *Guidelines* team. We hope to continue finding new talent and wisdom for this series, alongside our longstanding contributors.

We welcome two new contributors to this issue. Matthew Knell is a lecturer at London School of Theology and gives us one of our Advent readings this year. Jesus' story can become so familiar as to simply wash over us, so Matthew looks at some 'unexpected Advents' of Jesus to shake us awake to these surprising and joyful theophanies. We also welcome Ruth Bancewicz and her team from The Faraday Institute, who have collectively written two weeks of notes about God as creator. Each person contributes only one or two readings, but together they paint a picture of the wonder of creation and provide some fantastic ideas for how to engage with God through nature.

We are also pleased to welcome back contributors continuing their series from previous issues. Ashley Hibbard finishes off our journey through the Joseph cycle, as Joseph reunites with his brothers and then looks to the future. Steve Walton, who wrote on 1 Thessalonians in the previous issue, now completes the story by looking at 2 Thessalonians.

We also welcome back some other familiar faces. Stephen Finamore moves from Revelation to Romans as he explores the first four chapters of this dense book. Rosalee Velloso Ewell takes us on a tour of James, while Peter Hatton explores the difficulty of God's anger in Amos. As we enter Advent, David Spriggs introduces us to twin parables told by Jesus, and Henry Wansbrough brings us a week of notes on life after death. As we draw closer to Christmas, in addition to Matthew Knell's notes, Imogen Ball brings us to Christmas Day through an interesting exploration of the hymn 'O Come, O Come, Emmanuel'. We end the year in the company of Kate Bruce, who challenges us to think about nurturing, protecting and forming potential in children.

We hope you enjoy reading and engaging with this issue as much as we enjoyed putting it together. Our prayer is always that these notes and reflections would draw you closer to God.

Rachel Tranter and Olivia Warburton

The BRF Prayer

Almighty God,
you have taught us that your word is a lamp for our feet
and a light for our path. Help us, and all who prayerfully
read your word, to deepen our fellowship with you
and with each other through your love.
And in so doing may we come to know you more fully,
love you more truly, and follow more faithfully
in the steps of your son Jesus Christ, who lives and reigns
with you and the Holy Spirit, one God forevermore.
Amen

The BRF Centenary Prayer

Gracious God,
We rejoice in this centenary year
that you have grown BRF
from a local network of Bible readers
into a worldwide family of ministries.
Thank you for your faithfulness
in nurturing small beginnings
into surprising blessings.
We rejoice that, from the youngest to the oldest,
so many have encountered your word
and grown as disciples of Christ.
Keep us humble in your service,
ambitious for your glory
and open to new opportunities.
For your name's sake
Amen

See page 160 to find out more about BRF's centenary celebrations.

Genesis 44—50

Ashley Hibbard

In the May–August 2022 issue of *Guidelines*, we read through the first half of what is commonly called 'the Joseph cycle,' Genesis 37—43. These texts tell us the story of the events that led to the move of Jacob's family from Canaan to Egypt. This helps us to link the patriarchal narratives with the exodus from Egypt, the Old Testament's paradigmatic salvation story.

In this issue, we will continue our journey through this story, examining Genesis 44—50. While in the first half of the story the focus was mostly on Joseph, in the second half there is a much greater focus on Joseph's brothers: how will they respond to Joseph's final test? Are they changed men? And even if they are, how will Joseph respond to them? Will he save his family, or do his loyalties now lie with Egypt? Can they ever really be brothers again? These texts delve more into matters of intention, motivation and emotion than perhaps any other text in the Old Testament. These are people of deep feeling, unafraid to weep, to embrace, to complain, to rejoice. These chapters are deeply concerned with the complexity of human existence and relationship, the trouble that results from family discord and the difficulties of reconciliation and rebuilding trust. While hardly a prescription for how to deal with relational strife, these texts do us a great service by not giving us easy answers or simplistic solutions, while still portraying a largely positive outcome to the hardships of the past – all communicated in a story that is masterfully written and a pleasure to read.

Unless otherwise stated, Bible quotations are from the ESV.

1 The final test

Genesis 44:1–17

Joseph's final test is similar in means to his previous test, but it is different in scope. The first incident of the money in the sacks tested whether his brothers would report an error when no one was watching. In this test, Joseph makes the accusation of theft that they feared would be made the first time. First they were tested as to their honesty; now their reaction to false accusation is tested.

The matter of the 'stolen' cup being used for divination has troubled some readers of the text. Some have suggested that it is a lie, simply used to increase the significance of the missing cup. But the use of items to mediate supernatural forms of knowing was extremely common in the ancient Near East. Even though divination is later condemned in the law (Deuteronomy 18:10), Joseph precedes the law and so is not bound by it. Further, it seems that the definition of divination may have been narrower than it is today, as the casting of lots is used or referred to in both the Old and New Testaments (Joshua 7:14; Proverbs 16:33; Jonah 1:7; Acts 1:26), and these uses appear neutral at worst, and at times positive. Therefore it is not at all unreasonable or problematic to think that Joseph indeed uses this cup for some sort of spiritual or supernatural purpose.

Joseph probably chooses Benjamin as the one to implicate in the theft of the cup for a few reasons. First, given Jacob's favouritism, the risk of Benjamin's loss would cause the most fear among the brothers. Second, he is the only remaining child of Jacob's favoured wife, and thus perhaps of less significance to the other brothers, all of whom have at least one full brother. Finally, it is possible that Joseph has reasoned that if the brothers should fail this test, and are found to have so little regard for Benjamin that they would leave him behind, Benjamin would be safest remaining in Egypt under Joseph's protection.

Upon Benjamin's arrest, all the brothers return to Joseph, and this alone must have told Joseph much of what he needed to know about the change in his brothers' characters. In the last issue, I suggested that the brothers seem to have spent their lives 'looking over their shoulders', and here Judah alludes to a wrong they have done for which God is punishing them (v. 16).

2 A passionate plea

Although Judah interprets this difficult situation in which he and his brothers find themselves as a matter of divine retribution, he now demonstrates his nascent leadership and makes a plea to Joseph in what is arguably one of the Old Testament's greatest speeches. This monologue is the longest speech in the book of Genesis; in fact, it is longer than some of the narratives.

The primary hallmark of Judah's speech is humility. Thirteen times he refers to himself, his brothers or his father as 'your servant(s)'. While this is indeed an appropriately humble way to speak to a foreign power, in this constant use of the word Judah shows that he identifies himself and his family with Benjamin, the one who is facing enslavement. There is no blaming, othering or abandonment of this endangered brother.

He begins by recounting their first meeting with Joseph, highlighting the series of events that led to bringing Benjamin to Egypt (vv. 19–23). While there may be the slightest suggestion made that Joseph is responsible for Benjamin's presence in the first place, it can be forgiven for the incredible emphasis on Jacob's emotional fragility where Benjamin is concerned. This fragility then takes centre stage as Judah recounts the story of their return to Jacob (vv. 24–29). It is striking that he reports Jacob as saying, 'My wife bore me two sons.' While these exact words are not found in the text of Genesis 42:36—43:14, the sentiment is precisely correct. Judah recognises that he and Leah's other children are counted as little better than the maidservants' children, and it is a mark of his newfound humility that he acknowledges it apparently without resentment and instead focuses on his father's pain. Judah concludes all this with a statement that is unlikely to be hyperbolic, that he believes the loss of Rachel's second son would kill his father (vv. 30–32).

Judah concludes by offering his own life for Benjamin's. This is the reversal of Genesis 37: there, Judah recommended that they sell their brother as a slave. Here, Judah offers to take his brother's place as a slave.

3 The revelation

The chapter break between Genesis 44 and 45 is a poor one, as there is no shift in scene, and we are left hanging to learn what Joseph's response will be to Judah's impassioned speech. The break obscures the fact that Joseph's response is immediate and profound. Judah's offer to take Benjamin's place as a slave, probably combined with the emphasis in his speech on his father's pain and fragility, is too much for Joseph, who is now thoroughly convinced of his brothers' transformation.

Before he reveals himself, he sends his attendants away (v. 1). This is probably done in an effort not to lose face with his Egyptian staff. Though they knew that Joseph was Hebrew, his choice to hug foreign shepherds would probably be a bridge too far, as it was established earlier that there was something detestable about shepherds to Egyptians at this time in their history (43:32). As there is no evidence from Egyptian literature that shepherds were hated, Hartley (see further reading) speculates that this refers specifically to foreign nomadic herders who were distrusted by the Egyptians.

The brothers' response to Joseph's response is as strongly negative as his is positive. The word in verse 3 translated 'dismayed' might better be translated 'horrified'. It indicates the loss of all function due to overwhelming emotion or terror. They are both shocked that he is alive and terrified about what he might do to them.

While Joseph is honest about the impact of his brothers' wrongdoing, he quickly turns the discussion away from their guilt to God's good purposes. He says, 'God sent me before you' (v. 5), which in the immediate context foreshadows the family's move to Egypt, but in the broader context may also foreshadow Joseph as the first Hebrew slave in Egypt.

While the decision to reveal himself to his brothers appears to have been somewhat impulsive (v. 1), it is also evident that Joseph has been thinking about a longer-term plan and the needs of his family. Verses 7–13 and the emphasis both on divine purposes and the five years of famine that remain strongly suggest that all along he has hoped that his brothers had changed and his family could be saved. He tells them to report to their father about 'all my honour in Egypt' (v. 13), which would seem to be an oblique reference to the fulfilment of the dreams of his youth. This reunion ends with him weeping again and kissing Benjamin, as might be expected, but then he kisses all of them, a demonstration of his forgiveness.

4 Egypt offers refuge

While Joseph's revelation to his brothers began with him sending his attendants away for the sake of privacy and propriety, a report of Joseph's reunion with his brothers nonetheless reaches Pharaoh, who appears to be glad for him. While in his speech to his brothers Joseph tells them to come to Egypt and offers them his personal protection, here Pharaoh personally offers them the provision and protection of Egypt. This is somewhat ironic: while eventually Egypt will become the paradigmatic place of oppression and helplessness in the Hebrew Bible, there is a strong sense in Genesis of Egypt as a place of refuge.

Not only is Pharaoh glad for Joseph's reunion with and invitation to his family, but he is also surprisingly considerate and generous. Joseph's brothers return to Canaan with 20 donkeys loaded with food and 'good things of Egypt' (v. 23), as well as wagons, in order to make the journey more comfortable for their father and any others not able to walk long distances. This is more than just provision for a comfortable journey; it is also a demonstration of the resources that Egypt will be able to provide.

Most of these gifts come at Pharaoh's direction, but Joseph himself also gives gifts to his brothers: clothes, in particular. The significance of receiving garments from Joseph, stripped of his garment by his brothers, would surely not have been lost on them. Benjamin receives five changes of clothes, and a large sum of silver – again, an interesting reflection of the earlier story. The brothers sold Joseph and received a little silver, but Benjamin, who did not wrong him, receives much. Joseph's admonition not to fight on the trip home, a plea for unity, concludes this fascinating meeting, where Joseph's interaction with and gifts to his brothers serves as a sort of 'unmaking' of the events of Genesis 37.

Whereas Joseph was overcome with positive emotion at the sight of his brothers and at Judah's plea (45:1), and his brothers respond with tremendous fear (45:3), it is intriguing that when the brothers return to Jacob with news of his favoured son's survival, Jacob's response is numbness. It seems that this man who has grieved for countless years cannot summon the courage to hope that Joseph is alive, and it takes the brothers giving a full account to their father of the events in Egypt and the presentation of the provisions for the trip to make him believe at last.

5 The move to Egypt

Genesis 46:1–27

It has been established that moving to Egypt is Jacob's only option to save his family, from a human point of view, but it may also be that Jacob was somewhat reluctant to go. He travels as far as Beersheba, which is the southernmost point in the promised land, and spends the night there. While his grandfather Abraham had travelled to Egypt in a time of famine (12:10–20), his father Isaac had specifically been told not to go to Egypt during a famine (26:2–3). But here, in God's last appearance in Genesis, and his first direct appearance since Genesis 35, God reassures Jacob that this is the right thing to do, and that Jacob will indeed spend the rest of his life with his beloved son.

Verse 6 says that Jacob's family took with them 'their goods, which they had gained in the land of Canaan', but it seems likely that this represents only a fraction of the holdings that the family once had. Whereas Abraham was able to muster 318 men born in his house (14:14), the genealogy in this chapter lists a total of 70 people who went to Egypt. It is probable that the severity of the famine was such that the family needed to kill or sell much of their livestock, and also would have been unable to support unnecessary mouths to feed.

Following this is the only genealogical record in the Joseph cycle, and it records the names of Jacob's sons and grandsons, numbering those who journey with him to Egypt. In the broader context of the Pentateuch as a whole, this is probably intended to show what a relatively small community journeyed to Egypt and how greatly God blessed them in their time there, fulfilling his promise of a great nation to Abraham. There are few noteworthy features in this genealogy, but there is one item of particular interest. The last of Simeon's sons is said to be the son 'of a Canaanite woman' (v. 10). This is ironic behaviour from a man who was at the fore of the slaughter of a Canaanite city rather than see his sister married to a Canaanite (34:13–26). In fact, it is quite possible that since the brothers took women and children from the city as plunder (34:29), this Canaanite woman may in fact have come from Shechem.

6 Shepherds in Egypt

Genesis 46:28—47:12

In this section, Joseph's family arrives and settles in Egypt. We are told that Judah was sent ahead of the family. This detail is easily missed, but it is a reminder of the developing role of Judah in the Joseph cycle. In the earlier stories, he is an unrighteous leader, who persuades his brothers to sell Joseph and who acts selfishly and abusively towards his daughter-in-law. But his character arc becomes redemptive, apparently through Tamar's confrontation (38:26). This leadership that he demonstrates in the latter part of the Joseph narrative is what might be hoped for from God-honouring leaders: the sort that will act self-sacrificially for the good of others (44:18–34) and lead from the front (46:28). Judah has come to be a worthy ancestor of Israel's royal line.

Joseph's eagerness to see his father is demonstrated by his riding out to meet him in Goshen. Meeting his family there may have simply been a matter of convenience, as this is where Jacob's family would settle; on the other hand, if Goshen was located in the northeast of the Nile delta, this also meant that Joseph travelled as far as he could towards his father while still remaining in Egypt.

Joseph coaches his brothers somewhat about how to respond to Pharaoh's questions. If, as suggested previously, the Egyptians were suspicious of foreign herders, Joseph may be encouraging his brothers to double down on that fact in an effort to have them placed in a more remote location rather than in the major cities of Egypt, lessening the risk of assimilation into Egyptian society. Pharaoh thus arranges, as Joseph intends, to send Joseph's family to Goshen, away from the Egyptians who would likely have objected to the presence of foreigners when Egypt itself was in crisis. Pharaoh interviews Joseph's brothers and father and is especially solicitous of the latter, inquiring about his age and being blessed by him. While Joseph's aid to Egypt is certainly a blessing, it is nonetheless noteworthy to see the verb 'bless' (*barak*) used here. Abraham's grandson blesses a foreign power, the first overt incident of the blessing of the nations through Abraham's descendants (12:3).

Guidelines

There are many ways in which the book of Genesis prepares us for what follows in the Pentateuch and the Old Testament as a whole. One of these is an interest in rescue from Egypt. Egypt becomes a place of sorrow and enslavement, a place from which rescue is necessary, the place where God first showed his power. While in Genesis Egypt is a place of refuge and plenty in time of famine for both Abram (12:10–20) and for Jacob's family, we ought not miss the foreshadowing of enslavement. While Abram found refuge and plenty in Egypt, Sarai found herself subjected to a foreign power (12:15) and was only rescued by God's intervention. Joseph also is enslaved in Egypt and freed by a demonstration of God's power to interpret dreams. Jacob's family, though they at first find refuge, will later be enslaved, and rescued through God's power.

As we look across scripture for big themes and lessons, we do well to watch for the smaller stories, where we might see God making 'little promises' that foreshadow the larger, greater work. And as we look at our own lives and see God's faithfulness to us in what are ultimately small matters, let us use these moments to have confidence in his power to help us and comfort us in our times of desperate need.

1 Consequences of famine

Genesis 47:13–26

Immediately following Joseph's generous provision for his family to help them to survive the famine, we come to a story of a very different solution to the same problem. The people of Egypt also are out of food, and they buy food from the food stores that Joseph planned, losing their money, their livestock and their land. The Masoretic Text of verse 21 may also indicate an increase in the already present corvée labour that existed through much of Egyptian history, as it says of Joseph, 'As for the people, he relocated them to the cities from one end of Egypt's border to the other' (NASB).

Many commentators see in this text the unfolding of the severity of the famine. Hartley even suggests that Joseph's plan for sharecropping is quite just when compared to other similar systems of that time. But I am indebted here to Dr Helen Paynter, who first suggested to me that there may be a darker side to this story. Genesis 41:34 states that part of Joseph's counsel to Pharaoh was to reserve one-fifth of the produce of the good years to help Egypt survive during the famine. He calls the food 'a reserve for the land' (41:36). If that was truly the intent, why is Joseph selling this reserve to the Egyptian people? If his plan was to help the people, why would his plan cause the crown to profit from it but leave the people destitute?

While Joseph precedes the giving of the law and the ministry of the prophets, it is worth noting that what happens here is prohibited by the law of Jubilee, where all land was to revert to its ancestral owner (Leviticus 25:10). It seems that Israel was never faithful enough to see one of these Jubilees enacted, but that does not remove the intent of the law: that people should not be left without their inheritance in perpetuity. This is reinforced by Isaiah's oracle in Isaiah 5:8–9, where he pronounces woe over those who amass large tracts of property.

It may be that these interpretations are not mutually exclusive. It is possible that Joseph offered the Egyptian farmholders a better deal than might have been expected in the ancient world in similar situations. But it may also be that the composer of the text wanted to critique oppressive economic systems compounded by periodic unfree labour that would leave people unable to sit 'under [their] vine and under [their] fig tree' (Micah 4:4).

2 Joseph's sons, Jacob's sons

Genesis 47:27—48:22

For Jacob, little follows his relocation to Egypt except for the settling of his own affairs. He makes Joseph swear to him that he will take him back to Canaan to be buried (47:29–31). This may be because Joseph is his favourite, or perhaps because of God's promise to Jacob that Joseph will be with him when he dies. But he may also be unsure of how committed Joseph is to Canaan, a land in which he has not lived since his youth. He may be concerned that Joseph has assimilated into Egyptian culture, which explain why he doesn't accept at face value Joseph's agreement to return his body to Canaan, but extracts an oath.

Sometime after this oath, Joseph comes to Jacob with his sons Ephraim and Manasseh. Jacob reminds Joseph of the Abrahamic promise that God reaffirmed with Jacob at Bethel, focusing in particular on the promise of numerous descendants. This serves as a prelude to Jacob's request to Joseph: to give him his two eldest sons, so that they may directly benefit from God's promise to Jacob. Jacob says that Ephraim and Manasseh will be his 'as Reuben and Simeon are' (48:5). It is intriguing that he chooses specifically his two eldest sons to describe the place that Ephraim and Manasseh will have. Considering the disgrace into which Reuben and Simeon have fallen and the relatively minor tribes they will become, there is nearly a sense that Jacob is replacing them with these two grandsons. In this, he finds a way of giving a double portion to his favoured son, and we also ought not miss the irony that Jacob gives a double portion to the son who nearly had no inheritance at all. In response to this gift, Joseph, the second man of Egypt, bows to his father, in contrast not only to his great government power, but the grand dreams of his youth.

In 48:22, Jacob promises to Joseph 'one mountain slope'. The Hebrew word here is *shechem*, probably a reference both to the region and to the city that Jacob's sons captured and plundered in Genesis 34. In an irony that will shape the future of the nation of Israel and intertribal relationships, Simeon and Levi, who are the first to conquer a corner of the land of promise, do not themselves possess that land, but rather it is given to Joseph. The stolen and nearly murdered son, rather than his murderous brothers, receives the stolen, murdered city.

3 Jacob's blessing (1)

Genesis 49:1–12

Jacob's blessing to his sons is one of the most difficult texts in Genesis. It is written in verse and filled with wordplay that does not translate well into English. The meaning of many of the words is uncertain, and some of the phrases are rather unclear. Nevertheless, the blessings provide insight into some of the dynamics of the family, and in many cases appear to refer to the later characteristics for which the tribes would be known.

While we typically refer to this as the 'blessing' of Jacob's children, not all of what he has to say is positive or complimentary, and indeed his first three sons receive deeply condemning words. His words to Reuben acknowledge that he is literally the elder son, but reflect on Reuben's removal from the position and privilege that naturally would have accompanied that station, due to his sexual use of Bilhah, his father's concubine (35:22). Jacob's focus here is not so much on the personal dishonour that he suffered, but instead on the untrustworthiness that Reuben demonstrated and how that makes him unfit for family leadership (vv. 3–4).

Jacob's words to Simeon and Levi reflect on the leading role they played in the destruction of Shechem (34:25–26). Jacob distances himself from their actions and curses them with scattering, but how that plays out is very different (vv. 5–7). Simeon's territory is contained entirely within Judah's allotment (Joshua 19:1), and it appears that they may have been absorbed into Judah and lost a sense of tribal identity. Levi's curse becomes a blessing for the nation as a whole, as Levi receives no tribal allotment but rather cities in the midst of the other tribes, facilitating their ministry among the people. It is interesting that in the prior blessing, Jacob called Reuben 'turbulent' and 'unstable', and here he curses Simeon and Levi for their actions taken in anger. While it manifested differently, all three of these sons are disqualified from leadership for actions that, whatever else they may have been, show them to be unreliable.

Jacob's words to Judah are as positive as the prior words were negative. Judah is told that he will not only receive leadership of the family, but will receive 'the obedience of the peoples' (v. 10). He is depicted as receiving a dynasty and such unimaginable wealth that valuable items will become common (vv. 10–11). While glimmers of this are realised in David's dynasty and in particular in the reign of Solomon, Christians have from early times seen these words in a deeply Christological light.

4 Jacob's blessing (2)

Genesis 49:13–27

Except for the blessing to Joseph, this section of Jacob's blessing is concerned with the sons who have featured less prominently in the Joseph cycle, and who mostly will continue to lack prominence in the history of Israel.

Zebulun will be a coastal tribe, and the reference to a harbour implies wealth, but their territory will be nearly out of Israel (v. 13). Tracing the fulfilment of this is quite fascinating, for though Zebulun is among the first of the land to fall to the Assyrians, Isaiah prophesies that the Messiah will come in the land of Zebulun and Naphtali, in 'Galilee of the nations' (Isaiah 9:1).

Joseph receives the longest blessing, reflecting on his survival and endurance, and his tribe – in fact two tribes, both Ephraim and Manasseh – is blessed with those characteristics. 'Fruitfulness' is probably a wordplay referring to Ephraim's name, which means 'fruitful' (v. 22), and indeed 'Ephraim' becomes a synecdoche for the northern kingdom of Israel. The attacks depicted in verse 23 are probably a reference to the efforts of his brothers to destroy him, and what follows then may be a reference to Joseph's successes in Egypt: both God's presence with him far from home (v. 24), and the years of plenty, of which Joseph made wise use in order to save Egypt (v. 25). The final reference to 'set apart from his brothers' probably has a double meaning: slyly referring to Joseph's removal from his family by his brothers, but also to Jacob's honouring of him through adopting his eldest sons and thus giving him the double portion due to the eldest son (v. 26).

A brief blessing of Benjamin concludes this section, but it is oddly negative, perhaps looking ahead to the incident in Gibeah in Judges 19—21 and the near loss of the tribe (v. 27). This is a dark conclusion to a series of mostly positive blessings, and a sad outcome for a son who was so beloved by his father and his famous brother.

5 Jacob's death

Genesis 49:28—50:14

Upon the completion of his blessings to his sons, Jacob reiterates that he should be buried in Canaan, this time specifically referring to Abraham's purchase of the cave of Machpelah. This reference to Abraham, Sarah, Isaac, Rebekah and Leah (49:29–31) ties together the patriarchal narratives of Genesis. These are the last recorded words of the great patriarch, who then dies, as God promised, in the presence of his sons.

Perhaps more space is given to the description of Jacob's death rites than those of any other Old Testament figure. We see here a collision of cultures that is navigated in ways that are honouring both to Jacob's own culture and to the practices of the land in which his family finds itself. Joseph's decision to have his father embalmed is likely a way of showing honour to his father that the Egyptians would understand, and this is supported by the fact that the nation of Egypt observes a 70-day mourning period for this recently relocated foreign man (50:2–3).

Joseph pleads for Pharaoh's permission to let him return to Canaan to bury his father, being sure to promise to return. Even when Jacob's family moved to Canaan, and Joseph was to see his father for the first time in decades, Joseph did not leave the country, but only met his father at the border. Here, for the first and apparently only time since he was enslaved, Joseph returns to his homeland (50:5–7). This follows the motif of the patriarch's sons overcoming conflict to gather peaceably to bury their father (compare 25:9; 35:29).

The journey to Canaan is undertaken not only by Jacob's family, as would be expected, but also a great company of Egyptians (50:10). The journey almost has the feel of a pilgrimage, and the intense weeping from the Egyptian followers is a demonstration of the honour that the Egyptians have chosen to show to the father of the man who has saved them from famine. This whole scene is so improbable, and the weeping so conspicuous, that it is commemorated by a new Canaanite place name, 'the weeping of Egypt' (50:11).

6 Reconciliation at last

We see in this section what a difficult road reconciliation can be, and what a slow process it is to rebuild trust. Following their father's death, Joseph's brothers are afraid that Joseph has only been kind to them for the sake of their father. Perhaps they even wonder if this has all been an elaborate plot on Joseph's part to bring them to Egypt and so put them at his mercy. They send a message to Joseph, purportedly at Jacob's instruction, to ask his forgiveness, and this results in Joseph weeping once again. It is unclear exactly why he weeps. It may be that the reminders of what has happened are painful. It may be an expression of sorrow that his brothers do not trust him and felt it necessary to manufacture a command from Jacob. Similarly, he may be saddened that they feel it necessary to distance themselves from him, as they refer to themselves directly only as 'the servants of the God of your father' (v. 17) and 'your servants' (v. 18), leaving any reference to brotherhood on the (supposed) lips of Jacob (v. 17). These could also be tears of relief or joy that they have truly changed and humbled themselves enough to apologise. Likely it is a combination of all these reasons, and it overwhelms Joseph enough to cause him to weep. He summons his brothers, forgives them and reassures them of his goodwill.

The final verses are concerned with Joseph's death. While it was not surprising that Jacob wanted to be buried in Canaan, it is somewhat more surprising, and rather revealing, that Joseph insists that his body ultimately not be left in Egypt. Despite his Egyptian family, his mastery of the language, his relative caution in not appearing too close to his Canaanite brothers except in private and the largely Egyptian style in which he observes his father's death, we see here that Egypt has never become home. Yet it is also interesting that he does not ask to be taken immediately to Canaan and buried with his father. There are two possible reasons for this. First, he may believe that if he is buried in Egypt by Egyptians, the Egyptians will remember him longer and thus be more kindly disposed towards his family. The second option is more personal. His sons are in Egypt. His father's living family is in Egypt. And this man who spent far too much of his life far from his family may not want to be buried in a place where they are not.

Guidelines

Throughout scripture, extensive use is made of the images of homeland and exile. Much of the Old Testament is concerned with the land of Israel and the longing to find a home, maintain that home or return to it. But the New Testament largely turns these images on their heads and suggests that God's people are always 'sojourners and exiles' (1 Peter 2:11) and that God's faithful people have always looked for a heavenly city more than an earthly one (Hebrews 11:13–14).

Jacob describes the years of his life as 'few and evil' (47:9), even though he is speaking of sojourning in the land of promise. What a contrast to Joseph's contentment at a life spent far from home. Like Daniel much later, Joseph invests in the land in which he finds himself. He is able to remain faithful to God in the midst of a culture, value system and religious faith quite unlike his own, and he not only survives but flourishes, rising to the highest echelons of political power in this foreign land.

Sometimes Christians make use of the Egypt motif to describe life in a post-Christian society, and that is not without some merit. But let us remember that suffering and slavery are not the only options in such a context. God can use faithful people of courage and wisdom to bless both his kingdom and the earthly kingdoms in which we find ourselves. Our years don't have to be 'few and evil', if we but keep our eyes open for the opportunities to bless the nations that God has placed before us.

FURTHER READING

Joyce G. Baldwin, *The Message of Genesis* (IVP, 1996).

John E. Hartley, *Genesis* (Baker, 2000).

Gordon Wenham, *Genesis 16—50* (Word, 1994).

Romans 1—4:
unwrapping Romans

Stephen Finamore

It's about 25 years since Messiah Jesus rose from the dead. Paul and his team have been engaged in mission in the north-east quadrant of the empire for nearly two decades. The feeling is growing among them that they have done all they can in this area and that they are being called to something new. The team get together in Corinth to pray through the issues. They conclude that God is calling them to the north-west quadrant and, given the news of unrest in Gaul, they decide that they will begin work in Spain. There are a couple of things that need to be done before they can begin.

First, Paul has a significant promise to keep. When he met with the church leaders in Jerusalem, he promised to remember the poor. He had organised a collection among the churches he had planted, and the proceeds need to be delivered. Paul will have to go to Jerusalem.

Next, the team has really benefited from the support of the church in Antioch. They need to identify a church that can operate as a base of operations for the new mission to the west. The most westerly city where they have contact with significant numbers of Jesus' followers is Rome. It is agreed that Paul should write to them to introduce himself, arrange a visit and perhaps gently introduce the idea that they might support the new project.

But there are problems. First, Paul has never been to Rome. He has contacts there but does not know the situation first-hand. Second, there are divisions within the church there, some along ethnic lines. Finally, Paul is not always understood properly, either by those who claim to follow him or by those who oppose him. He will have to set out his position on a range of sensitive issues if he is to help the church unite and commit itself to supporting the work in Spain.

Unless otherwise stated, Bible quotations are taken from the NRSV.

1 Paul introduces himself

Romans 1:1–7

Paul begins his charm offensive. Aware that a significant number of the Roman followers of Jesus are not free, he calls himself the slave of King Jesus. He is identifying himself with those with the lowest social status. Then, just in case any have misunderstood and have seen the gospel about Jesus as a wholly new thing, unconnected in any way to the story of God's people up to this point, Paul makes it clear that it flows out of God's words through the prophets of Israel. He then sets out the gospel, something he shares with the listeners, using words they are familiar with and carrying links with established Jewish understandings of Christianity. Then Paul states his understanding of his own ministry. Some might have expected him to speak of bringing faith to the nations, but he chooses to express the ethical dimension of his thinking by using the word 'obedience'. And then he greets all the people of God in Rome.

When Paul summarises the gospel, he does not tell it as a series of propositions, although it includes a number of these. Instead, he tells a story, and he tells it using terms that would have been familiar to his audience, in this case the Jewish and Judaism-influenced followers of Jesus in Rome. There are lessons here for us about the use of narrative and taking context seriously.

A colleague in church ministry told me how difficult he found it to explain what he does, especially in a secular context. Paul was able to give a succinct account of his own calling. Perhaps his example can help us to do the same.

2 Paul's desires for God's people in Rome

Romans 1:8–17

It's traditional to include a thanksgiving section in a letter like this, but Paul is wholehearted in his appreciation of these groups who maintain the faith in the very heart of the empire. He really does want to visit them. He talks about it a great deal. He believes he can help strengthen the church by encouraging them to be united. He's also aware that he did not found the church and is not its leader, and so there must be some mutuality in the learning. Paul knew he was called to all the nations of the world, those who regarded themselves as part of the Greek-speaking world and those from beyond; those who were educated and those who were untrained. These groups could all be found in Rome, and so Paul was anxious to visit and to share Jesus there. Paul understood that Rome – the capital of the empire, the centre of its communications network and the place where representatives of nations from all over the world were gathered – would be a great base of operations for the next stage of his mission.

Then Paul sets out the theme of his letter – the gospel that can bring salvation to everyone. He names the categories in the chronological order of hearing from or about Jesus – first the Jewish people, then the rest. This message is about God's action to secure salvation. For Paul, salvation means the process through which the world is put back on to a path that will lead it to the goal that God had originally intended. This involves the action that restores relationships with God, with others and with the whole of creation. Paul says that the gospel reveals the righteousness of God. He means that what God has done in Messiah Jesus is to keep his ancient promises, the things he bound himself to do in his covenant with his people. In the gospel, God has revealed his own character in all its integrity. He is faithful, through and through. Habakkuk makes the case: God's people live in trust in God's promises. The prophet was concerned about the rise of the Babylonians who were known for their terrible violence. He was sure that God ought to act to keep his promises to protect his people. God responds that his people, those who are in a right relationship with him, live in faithful trust.

There is so much in the world that makes us anxious. It is quite right that we should be concerned about some of them: the threat of war, the environmental crisis, the decline of the church in the west, to name a few. However, our concern should never undermine our trust that God is faithful and will keep all his promises.

3 God's action to ensure justice

'Wrath' is not a popular word. Yet Paul insists that the revelation of wrath and the revelation of righteousness are two sides of the same coin. Lots of us struggle when we hear the word 'wrath' used about God. Some rightly point out that in other letters it is included in lists of things to be avoided. However, it seems that Paul uses this word in at least two ways. Sometimes it describes the kind of angry response to others that is always inappropriate. On other occasions it has a more technical meaning. Wrath, when applied to God or even to human authorities, is the steadfast determination that a judge needs to ensure that justice is done. If you look at it this way, then you cannot have justice without wrath. Paul is arguing that humankind as a whole has behaved in a way that is contrary to God's purposes and to God's justice. As a good judge, committed to doing right, God experiences wrath, the motivation to pursue justice.

So how have humans gone wrong? Collectively, humankind allowed their desires to become distorted. They gave ultimate value to the seen rather than to the unseen, to the created rather than to the uncreated, to images rather than to reality. This distortion had consequences. It started with the inward person but soon impacted the outward. Essentially, humankind's failure to make God the focus of their desire, their worship and their lives led to distortions in their understandings, which caused moral chaos. The worst of it was that they couldn't even see it. Paul is not simply describing something that happened once; he is stating a principle for the way human social life works. If God ceases to be at the centre of human existence, the eventual result is moral chaos in which people stop being able to tell wrong from right. Make no mistake, God will ensure that justice is done.

Some of us may struggle with these sorts of ideas, but Paul is quite deliberately establishing common ground with his readers, especially the ones with a Jewish background and those who were non-Jews who had associated themselves with the synagogue. They knew that one of the ways the scriptures understand God is as a judge. And as a judge, he would ensure that justice was done.

4 Take care before you agree!

Romans 2:1–11

Lots of people in Paul's audience would probably have agreed with every word of Paul's statements about God's wrath. They would have said that it was a good summary of everything that was wrong with their neighbours. The sooner God sorted them out, the better! Paul had no time for this kind of self-righteous person, and in these verses he makes it clear that, like it or not, they are caught up in the same issues. One of Paul's techniques was to address an imaginary listener and hold a dialogue with them. He introduces someone who broadly agrees with what has been said so far. He probably has in mind someone Jewish or with strong links to the synagogue. This person imagines that Paul's argument applies to the nations but not to Israel, or to others but not to themselves. Paul wants to challenge exactly this.

Israel or some parts of it, and the church as well, must learn that God is judge and we are not. If part of Israel has turned their back on God, this means that they too will be judged by God. The same rules apply to both the Jews and the Greeks. On this point God is impartial. Paul's point is that it is not enough simply to be Jewish. You have to live as the Jews are supposed to live. Paul continues to use the idea of God as a judge and claims that there will come a day when everyone must face judgement. Anyone who lives as God intended will receive the promised honour and peace. Anyone who does not will face tribulation and distress. The judgement will not be based on 'one rule for you and one rule for me' but on God's original purposes for all humankind. Therefore, Jews, or Gentiles who attend the synagogue, who do not live as God had taught them will get the same outcome as anyone else who lives like that. It's worth noting that the glory and honour to be received by those who do live as God intends is, according to Psalm 8:5, exactly what God has planned for people from the beginning.

Once again, the Bible teaches us to be very careful about judging others and encourages us to examine our consciences to see if we are living in the way God wants. It is presumption and complacency that Paul has in his sights. At the time his chosen conversation partner was someone associated with Judaism, but today he might well have targeted someone proud of their role and status in Christian mission and ministry.

5 It's doing the law, not knowing it, that matters

Romans 2:12–24

Paul is making a point about the Torah, the Instruction, which we tend to call the law. This was God's great gift to the Jewish people. However, possessing the law does not mean that you are approved by God. The purpose of the law was not that you should possess it or even that you should know it, though both are obviously good things. The point of the law was that you should be transformed by it and live it. In the end, it will be those who perform the law who will be the redeemed people of God. Imagine, says Paul, a group of people who do not know the law but who do it anyway. Obviously, they would be part of God's people. Some think that Paul is being hypothetical here or that he is imagining a righteous Gentile group somewhere. I believe that it is far more likely that Paul is thinking about Gentile Christians. They may not possess the law but, because of the presence of God's transforming Spirit in their lives, they live out the true purpose of the law. The corollary of the argument is that a person who does know the law but doesn't do it will not be considered part of God's people. The problem with the synagogue is that it contains people who teach the law but tolerate within their ranks people who break the law in the ways Paul mentions.

Earlier, Paul said that God 'will repay according to each one's deeds' (2:6) and here he says it is 'the doers of the law who will be justified' (v. 13). These texts trouble some of us because they don't clearly state the idea of salvation by faith alone. However, Paul will not allow the idea of being justified to be separated from the idea of being part of the people of God, and he is sure that the people of God are the people who live as God intended. Faith in Christ is the thing that justifies us and therefore makes us part of God's people and brings us the Spirit to enable us to live in a particular way and to put the law's requirements into our hearts. But if the living bit isn't happening at all, something is amiss.

6 The badge of circumcision

Romans 2:25–29

Throughout the letter to the Romans, Paul is concerned with the people he calls Israel. He addresses the issue in depth in chapters 9—11. However, the issue crops up several times, in different ways, in the preceding chapters. Israel matters because it is a way of talking about the people of God. In Romans, Israel is described in several ways. Most obviously, Israel consists of the people called Jews. The Jews are the people to whom God's law has been given, so they are the people who possess the law and who are under the law. In addition to this, there is a sign, mark or badge for the males who belong to this group. It is a symbol of belonging, and it is called circumcision. When Paul discusses circumcision, the law, being Jewish and being Israel, the arguments are inevitably closely related. The Hebrew scriptures know that the law and circumcision are wonderful gifts and privileges, and Paul, as a Jewish man, knows this is true. However, the scriptures also know that circumcision can become an empty symbol and that's why they speak of a necessary circumcision of the heart (Deuteronomy 10:16; 30:6), just as it's the reason the prophets foresee a time when the law will be written on the hearts of God's people (Jeremiah 31:33).

Imagine you buy a car. It has a Rolls Royce badge on it. When you get it home and open the bonnet, you see that it does not have the right engine. The badge and the reality do not match. Circumcision is a sign that someone is part of God's people and is great provided you live that way. But if you don't, then it's actually misleading. Truly being a part of the people of God is not something marked outwardly but marked inwardly; it is a matter of the heart.

It is important for us not to rely on our badges or status symbols. Our clerical collars, fish badges and so on may have their uses, but if they are not matched by a particular way of life, then they are worse than useless. Paul insists that when push comes to shove, what matters is the way we live.

Guidelines

Paul has introduced himself and offered an outline of his message and his reasons for writing. Next, he has stated the great theme of the letter, the gospel that reveals God's righteousness. Paul begins the exposition of his theme by summing up the human dilemma: distorted desire has led to idolatry, which has created moral chaos, which means humans find themselves faced with God's demand for justice. There might be parts of humanity who think this analysis applies to others and not to themselves. Paul takes on this group and demonstrates that every category of human faces God's justice on the same basis.

- Think again about Paul's critique of the human condition. What language would you use to sum up the state we're in? What was it that led us down this path?
- Write down a succinct summary of the gospel and of your own role in ministry, mission and discipleship.
- What are the issues that concern you so much that they might challenge the call to trust in God's promises? Is there anything going on in the world or in the church that makes you despair and lose hope or perspective?
- Are there times you can remember when you pointed a finger in judgement at others only to later realise that you could (perhaps should) have been talking to yourself?
- Sometimes people see a tension between the idea of salvation through faith alone and the ethical demands of the gospel. How do you resolve that tension?
- Are there any symbols or positions that you rely on to claim a special status with God? Is there anything that needs to change in this area?

Give thanks to God who has acted in Jesus to save us from the consequences of our own actions.

1 The judgement of God

Romans 3:1–20

Paul is still talking to his imaginary conversation partner. They are wondering, given what Paul has just said, whether there's really any point to being Jewish. Paul insists that there is, but just not in the way that some people believe. Just because some Jews were unfaithful doesn't mean that God is – he remains faithful to all his promises, especially those made to his covenant people. This is something that Paul will explore in depth later in the letter. Nevertheless, the main point that Paul is making here is that the whole of humankind, Jew and Gentile alike, have not lived in accordance with God's original purposes. Instead, they live under the power of sin. That is, as we saw earlier, they live in the realm where desire and purpose have been distorted and, as a result, humans are unable to live in the way that God intended and so are unable to attain to the goals for which they were created.

This was certainly true for the nations of the world, but it was also true for God's own people. Paul quotes a whole chain of texts to make his point. Each text insists that its readers have departed from God's ways. These words all come from the scriptures given to the Jews, so they, like the Gentiles, have no grounds for being considered part of God's people. The things that make you ethnically Jewish, like circumcision and keeping the food laws, are not enough to make you part of God's redeemed people. The law itself tells us this. Therefore, every part of humankind, having failed to live as God intended, is subject to the wrath of God. This means that God, understood as a judge, in his concern for justice, is determined to set an appropriate penalty.

So, those who have the law live under the power of sin and are, or should be, aware of it. Those, like the Gentiles, who live without the law, are also under the power of sin, but are probably not aware of it. One of the things the law does is to let you know the state you are in. After all, if you don't have a commandment, you don't know you're breaking it. This means that Jews and Gentiles are in the same situation, but that Jews should be more aware of it.

In a similar way, the scriptures have much to teach us about ourselves and the society we live in. Our churches should therefore be well placed to help others understand the human condition and speak truthfully about it in a similar way to the biblical prophets.

2 The solution of God

Romans 3:21–26

As we have seen, God's wrath, his desire to see justice done, means that every part of humankind is subject to the same sentence. According to Psalm 8, glory was God's goal for humans. Sadly, every part of humankind has come up short. Nevertheless, God remains faithful to his original purposes for his creation. Paul may once have taught that God would keep his promises through the law. Perhaps he believed that if all the Jewish people could be persuaded to keep the law properly, God would act to redeem Israel. Paul now realised that God had kept his covenant promises in a different way, though the scriptures saw it coming. God had kept his promises through the faithfulness of Messiah Jesus, and this was for all who were loyal to him, whether they were Jew or Gentile. All had failed to live in the way that God intended but all can become part of God's people through what God has done in Jesus. Through him, God had dealt with human wrongdoing so that those who now follow him can be part of the people of God.

Through Jesus, particularly through his lifeblood, by which Paul means his faithful obedience to the Father even to the point of death, God has dealt with sin and therefore with wrath. This means that the whole of creation can get back on track and develop into the cosmos that God always intended it to become. Paul uses a temple image to make his point. This was where the ritual was carried out that symbolised not only the cleansing of God's people, but the restoration of the whole of creation. Paul refers to God presenting Jesus as the mercy seat, which was situated on the top of the ark of the covenant in the holy of holies. This was the place where the blood of the sacrifice was sprinkled on the Day of Atonement and the place where the divine presence was manifested. Since Paul refers to Jesus' blood, we should understand that the cross of Jesus was a manifestation of God's presence as well as an event that achieved atonement and restoration.

The wrath of God is a tricky idea for many. Lots of us have friends who struggle to sing hymns that refer to it. It's important to remember that in Paul's thought it is always related to God's role as judge and to his desire to bring about justice.

3 Some preliminary conclusions

There's no room for making out that we've achieved anything by ourselves. Some people today boast about their nationality and talk as though their ethnic group is exceptional or more significant than other people's. This is a form of boasting. It's a way of stressing your differences from others. Paul is very keen on his own national identity. However, he works hard to keep it in perspective. Being Jewish doesn't automatically put you in God's good books. It appears that some of Paul's fellow Jews presumed that their national identity was a guarantee of God's favour and that it was appropriate to boast about this. Paul doesn't agree. The people he is arguing with often claim that the law backs them up, but Paul takes a different view.

Paul distinguishes between a law of works and a law of faith. He'll have more to say about this later. Basically, the law of works might support the case of his opponents. It is focused on outward signs and genetic descent. But the law of faith is about the inner person and spiritual identity. Paul insists that this is the thing that matters. Essentially, the argument is about how you define the people of God. Is it something outward? Or something inward?

Paul's opponents say that genetic descent from Abraham is the basis for belonging to the people of God. Paul says that following Messiah Jesus defines the people of God. They are the ones who are justified. This is courtroom language. Paul means that it is declared in the present that this group of people will be vindicated at the final judgement. This group belongs to the covenant people of God, not because they maintain any markers of their ethnic background but because they are loyal to Jesus. Paul insists that if ethnic markers did the trick, then you could argue that God is God of Jews alone, but we know that's not true. Jewish people belong to God's people because of their loyalty to Jesus, and so do non-Jewish people. And, Paul insists, this does not undermine the law in any way. In fact, it upholds it! Ethnicity matters, but it is not the basis of belonging to God or to his people.

Patriotism can be a positive thing, and there is an appropriate love of one's own people and traditions. However, if this slips into the exclusion of those who are different or into feelings of superiority over others or if it becomes a justification for territorial expansion, it has become a false idol. As Paul insists, God is God of the whole world and is not the exclusive preserve of any one people.

4 It all started with Abraham

Romans 4:1–8

Paul still has in mind the issue of Jews and Gentiles. He is aware that Jewish people claim descent from Abraham and that some think this gives them a secure status with God. Now he's going to make a challenging point. When God made his great promise to Abraham and declared that he was considered to have righteousness – which is to say, he was regarded as living the life that God intended for all humankind and that he was part of, or perhaps the beginning of, the covenant people of God – Abraham was not a Jew. He was not circumcised, and he did not have the law. Of course, neither was he a non-Jew – a Gentile – because the distinction did not yet exist. It's the promise that matters and not the line of descent. Abraham is the spiritual ancestor of all those who trust in God.

Abraham is declared to be justified. This is a legal term indicating that a judge has found in your favour in a courtroom context. God is the judge, and a day will come when he judges the world (2:16). God has promised to find in favour of those who live as he intended. And he has told Abraham, well in advance of the day of judgement, that the verdict will be in his favour. This means his wrongdoings are forgiven and that he is part of God's covenant people. This was not something Abraham deserved or had earned. It was a matter of God's abundant generosity.

God remains generous and so this gift of welcoming the undeserving into his covenant people is something that remains available today. It is a gift that comes to us through our faithful dependence upon God and the things he has done for humankind through Messiah Jesus.

One of the issues with the words 'faith' and 'belief' is that they can imply intellectual consent and nothing more. This is an important part of Paul's meaning but not all of it. His use of the terms implies trust and dependence. It's been suggested that to have faith in someone is to pledge them your allegiance.

5 God's people trust in God's promises

Romans 4:9–15

The blessing of God that made Abraham part of God's covenant people came before there was ever a distinction between Jews and non-Jews. It didn't happen because Abraham had been circumcised. It happened because God is generous and chose to regard Abraham's trust in his promises as the basis for accepting him. When Abraham was subsequently circumcised, it was a sign of the acceptance he had already received. Therefore, Abraham is the spiritual ancestor of all the people of God, whether they are Jewish or not.

We usually interpret the promise to Abraham and his descendants in terms of the land he was promised. Paul seems to understand the land as standing for something greater – the whole of the earth. If the promise to Abraham and his offspring was that all the nations of the world would be blessed through them, then the promise of the land must have a similar extent. That's why Paul says in verse 13 that Abraham's seed will inherit the earth. Paul believes that this seed is Messiah Jesus and those who follow him. They are, in Jesus' words, the meek who will inherit the earth. In other words, the people of God are those who trust in God's promises, not those who rely on circumcision and the law.

In fact, there is a connection between law and wrath, that is, between the Torah and God's action to ensure that justice is done. This is something Paul will explore in greater depth later in the letter. The point is that if you don't have a commandment, you can't disobey it. As the Jewish people are the ones who know God's commands, they're the ones who are aware when they transgress and as a result are the ones who ought to know that they face God's wrath.

6 Trusting in Jesus is life out of death, creation out of nothing

Romans 4:16–25

The promises are for all the spiritual descendants of Abraham, whether they are Jews or non-Jews. Abraham, though he made many mistakes, lived his life in a way that showed he trusted in the promises of God. He put his focus on God rather than on his and Sarah's own circumstances. It is this kind of trust, this kind of allegiance, that makes us part of God's covenant people. It was true for Abraham, and it is true for us.

God is the one who can make something out of nothing. He is the one who brings life from the dead. He brought Isaac from the good-as-dead bodies of Abraham and Sarah. He brought Messiah Jesus back from the dead. Jesus was handed over to be executed because of all the times when we went against the known purposes of God. And he was raised from the dead so that we might be part of God's people and so know that, when the judgement comes, God will find in our favour.

It's wonderful that God can take the nothingness of our lives and bring positive things out of it. He has taken all our wrongdoings and carried them away in the death of Jesus. If we place our trust in him, we need have no fear of death or judgement but can fully embrace the life God offers.

Guidelines

Paul has explained that whoever we are, Jew and non-Jew – but this would apply to other categories too – we are all in the same boat. There is no part of humankind that has lived life in the way God intended and so, in God's courtroom, there is no case for the defence. However, despite human wrongdoing, God has chosen to be true to himself, to his original purposes for creation and to his covenant promises. He has accomplished this through Messiah Jesus, whom he gave as a sin-offering. At first sight, this might seem to go against God's own law. However, if you read the stories carefully, you'll find that they do not teach that the law can make you part of the covenant people of God. Instead, they reveal that God's people have always consisted of those who live trusting in his promises.

- We often read of people who live with a sense of entitlement. Perhaps you know some who take this attitude with God. What would Paul say to them?

- Paul was, of course, very proud of his Jewish heritage. Nevertheless, some think his arguments undermine the status of Jews in their own stories and traditions and so justify anti-Semitism. Can Paul be defended against this charge?

- The apostle makes his case based on certain texts, especially Genesis 15. Are there other texts that give less support to his argument?

- Does it help or hinder our understanding of Paul if we understand his use of the word 'faith' as meaning – among other things – allegiance to the Lord Jesus?

- To what extent are you living in a daily dependence on the promises of God? Remind yourself of any times when you trusted in God when all your outward circumstances cried out for a different strategy.

Give thanks that God generously offers forgiveness and life to those who trust in him.

Our creator God

Ruth Bancewicz

We inhabit an incredible planet, where great beauty, fruitfulness and diversity can be found even in the most surprising places. An ordinary urban garden, railway embankment or field edge may contain countless species of insects, plants and microbes. Deep sea vents or subterranean caves can be bursting with life. We benefit from creation in countless ways, including food, drink, clothing, medicine, building materials and relaxation. There is also a messy side to the non-human world – a wildness that we have to learn to live alongside, as well as the pain, disease and environmental destruction that can result from our own broken relationship with the created order.

The next two weeks' studies were written by people with a great deal of experience in studying God's world using the tools of science. A number have studied theology formally and/or taken part in in-depth discussions of science and religion, and all have benefited from years of thoughtful engagement with the Bible and service in the church. We will work through some of the familiar passages on creation that are scattered throughout the Old and New Testaments, but with a different slant. Each writer has shared some of their own heart for scientific exploration in a way that helps unpack the meaning of the passage.

The aim of this series is to demonstrate how a scientific perspective can expand and enhance our view of God as creator, both individually and corporately. I hope you find these studies encouraging and uplifting, expanding your mind to take in a little more of the God of the whole universe and his creative attributes.

Unless otherwise stated, Bible quotations are taken from the NIV.

1 Creator

Keith Fox

Hebrews 1:1–4

Some people may be surprised to think of Christ as the creator, but that's what we read in this passage and in other parts of scripture, such as the opening verses of John's gospel: 'Through him all things were made; without him nothing was made that has been made' (John 1:3). We cannot draw clear lines between the activities of the three persons of the Trinity. What one person does, they each are involved with, and the whole of the Trinity was involved in the act of creation – it was that important!

Not only did Christ make the world, but he is heir of everything – everything was made for him. It's easy to think and act as if God made everything for our benefit, but that's not so; it was made for Christ and to show his glory. That includes many things in the far-flung corners of the universe that we cannot begin to imagine and that human eyes will never see. These were all made for him, as his inheritance. Everything was made by Christ and for him. Of course, 'all things' includes you and me as well.

Science is very good at explaining how the world works and we can measure and predict how things behave with repeatable scientific laws. God has ordered the world so that we can study the way that it works. Although there is still much to discover, we now understand many things, from the immense size of the universe to the wonder of the human body and the intricate workings inside each of our body's cells. It can therefore be tempting to think that this all occurs by 'natural' processes, but Christians affirm that nature does nothing by itself.

Above all these things, and underpinning them, is Christ. As today's passage says, he is 'sustaining all things by his powerful word' (v. 3). We see things as regular and natural because that is the way God has ordered his creation, and we are privileged to study the way it works. But that is only possible because of his ongoing sustaining power. God didn't just make the universe and everything in it and then walk away, waiting for his inheritance to mature. He is intimately involved with it, sustaining all things by his powerful word; not just propping it up, but lovingly looking after everything moment by moment.

2 Creative

Rodney Holder

Proverbs 8:22–31 (NRSV)

This great hymn to personified wisdom tells us that wisdom precedes the creation and is at God's side as a 'master worker' as the creation unfolds (v. 30), translating the Hebrew *āmōn*, which could alternatively be read as 'little child'. We see God's wisdom in the creation when we look up at the night sky, view a mountain landscape, see the sea or watch a bird. The sciences help us to explore this wisdom in detail. Indeed, it is often a sense of deep awe at the universe which motivates such study. The unfathomable richness of creation is revealed when, as typically occurs, we answer one question, only for more questions to open up. Wisdom herself delights in living creatures and especially in human beings. As Shakespeare puts it, 'What a piece of work is a man! How noble in reason! How infinite in faculty!'

The root meaning of the verb *qānāh,* translated 'created' (v. 22), is 'got', and is used in Genesis 4:1 of Eve bearing Cain: 'I have produced [i.e. got] a man.' Thus wisdom can be conceived as God's child. The noun *derek*, translated 'work', primarily means 'way' and 'beginning of his way' can be taken as 'firstborn'. The verb translated 'brought forth' in verses 24 and 25 also has the connotation of 'to travail in childbirth'. It is thus no surprise perhaps that the New Testament sees Christ as God's wisdom; indeed he is named as such in 1 Corinthians 1:24 and as firstborn in Colossians 1:15. These ideas were developed by the Church Fathers through much discussion of today's passage. The Arians could also use the passage by adopting the 'created' meaning. However, both Origen and Athanasius drew a distinction between creating and begetting, and understood the latter as an eternal act so that there never was when the Son was not.

The idea of Christ as the Word of God, which we meet in the prologue to John's gospel, resonates with this passage, since the word *Logos* is also the Greek for 'reason', and for the Greeks the *Logos* was the ordering principle of the universe (though Irenaeus kept the distinction, seeing the Word and Wisdom as God's hands in creation). Knowing the architect, let us rejoice ever more in his creation, just as he does himself.

3 Sustainer

Denis Alexander

The context of this passage is that one of Job's 'comforters', Bildad the Shuhite, has just been telling him that the godless are like reeds that whither without water. But, Bildad says, if Job pulls his socks up, then everything will work out alright in the end. These rather banal comments are met by this fine speech by Job.

Here is no distant deistic god who winds up the universe at the beginning and then just lets it run by itself, but the theistic God who sustains and upholds all that exists. The works of God seem like miracles to us (v. 10), not as in philosopher David Hume's idea that they involve the 'breaking of laws of nature', but simply in their sheer wonder. Staring at the night sky on a clear night – especially away from city lights – can provide that immediate sense of awe at God's creation, with its hundred billion (100,000,000,000) galaxies, each one containing around a hundred billion stars on average (give or take a few).

Job's understanding of creation is entirely consistent with what we read about creation in the rest of the Bible. And out of this understanding came the overthrow of Aristotelian science that was such a key aspect of the scientific revolution of 16th- and 17th-century Europe. The earlier Aristotelian approach was that nature was ordered according to the intrinsic properties of natural things. Objects in the natural world have essences and inherent goal-directed tendencies that govern their behaviours. It is in the *physis,* or essence, of stones to fall downwards and for flames to go upwards. So just observe, thought Aristotle, and common sense will do the rest. But the early scientists ('natural philosophers'), nearly all Christians, said that physical things are artefacts made by God – nature is not a self-organised and goal-directed living thing. The only way you can find out how material things work is by doing experiments. Out of this theistic conviction of God as creator and moral law-giver also came the idea of scientific laws.

So the Jewish conviction about the great all-powerful and involved creator God, so vividly described here by Job, was destined to help change the world through science.

4 Provider

Sarah Perrett

Psalm 104:1, 10–18, 24–30

This psalm celebrates God's creation and begins with a call to worship the creator (v. 1). As a scientist, I study the world that God has created and my work is worship. If I separate my Christian faith and my secular work, then not only does the work become dry, but my soul does too. Isn't this true for any of us, whether our work is 'sacred' or 'secular', whether outside the home or inside the home, whether we receive a salary or not?

God not only created the earth and all its living creatures, but he also made the earth produce all that is required to sustain his creation. Notice the emphasis on abundant water, which is essential for all the plants and animals to survive (vv. 10–13). From there comes the grass for cattle to eat and plants for people to cultivate for food (v. 14). We now know that it is the green plants that capture carbon dioxide from the air which produces not only food, but also the oxygen we breath. Cultivating the fruit of the earth provides purpose and pleasure for humankind (v. 10–15). The well-watered trees provide a nesting place for birds and the mountain crags provide a home for animals (vv. 16–18). God has provided the earth as a resource so that we and all his creatures can thrive. Do we treasure this? Do those of us who live in well-watered places show concern for those who are suffering the effects of man-made climate disaster?

As I study God's works in the lab, I am humbled by the richness of his wisdom and feel awe at the vastness and variety of his creation (vv. 24–26). We are completely dependent on God, both for the good things he gives us for practical day-to-day living (vv. 27–28) and for life (or death) itself (vv. 29–30). Do we acknowledge this in the way we live? Do we separate sacred from secular and deprive ourselves from tapping into God's treasure trove of wisdom? Or do we ask him to guide us in our daily decisions, knowing that he can see beyond the horizon?

5 Faithful

Hugh Rollinson

Genesis 9:8–17

It is perhaps surprising to see how broad God's covenant with Noah is, for it not only encompasses Noah's family and his descendants but all creatures – birds, domesticated animals and even the wild animals that might otherwise be seen as a threat (vv. 9–10). We don't often focus on God's care for animals, and yet mammals, birds and reptiles have lived on land for at least the last 200 million years and forms of marine life for much longer. No wonder animals have a special place in God's thinking even to the point at which they are part of the worshipping community of heaven (Revelation 4:8).

And yet we live in times of crisis. The recent Dasgupta Report on the Economics of Biodiversity states that 'biodiversity is declining faster than at any time in human history'. In the introduction to this report, David Attenborough writes, 'Today, we ourselves, together with the livestock we rear for food, constitute 96% of the mass of all mammals on the planet. Only 4% is everything else. We are destroying biodiversity, the very characteristic that until recently enabled the natural world to flourish so abundantly.' A number of recent authors have highlighted that it is our modern patterns of consumption that are the root of this decline; these are manifest in our approaches to land use (for food production) and climate change (our demand for cheap energy).

So how does this square with our reading from Genesis and God's declared covenant commitment of care for the whole animate world (v. 10)? We have God's promise that never again will all life be destroyed, reaffirming the original importance of animal life on Earth as an essential part of God's creation. This promise has the whole character of God behind it – this is a promise that cannot be broken – as is confirmed by the sign of the rainbow. Further, this is a promise for all generations (v. 12) and so is just as relevant in our times as it was in the days of Noah.

Today we see God's concern for biodiversity loss being worked out through those groups and governments seeking to protect the natural environment. Last year I visited a farm in South Africa where the (Christian) farmer is seeking to reintroduce on to his land the world's most illegally trafficked animal – the pangolin. Closer to home are Christian organisations working to fulfil God's re-creation mandate found in today's verses (see Further reading on p. 52).

6 Wise

Robert White

Job 38

Today's passage focuses on the wisdom and the sovereignty of the creator. God is addressing Job, who had been through a terrible time, losing his wealth, his health and all ten children. Job just wanted God to explain why the world could be so tough, especially when Job himself was a believer who put his trust in God – and God himself acknowledged Job's righteousness.

God's response as he speaks 'out of the storm' (v. 1) is to point to the magnificence of his creation, which lies all around us. This chapter and the next two from the book of Job beautifully explain God's immense creativity, his power and his sovereignty. Every single thing in the entire universe was called into being by God himself. That extends from the vastness of the universe itself (vv. 4–5, 8) and the uncountable stars it contains (vv. 7, 31–33) to the smallest details of providing food for the young lions and ravens (vv. 39, 41). God is sovereign over the scary chaos of the sea (vv. 8–11), and even the underworld, the place of death itself, is not outside his knowledge and control (v. 17).

There is deep irony in God's questioning of Job as he points out all these things he created and over which he has sovereignty: 'Tell me, Job, if you understand' (v. 4); 'Surely you know!' (v. 5). By implication that includes us too. We may think we are immensely clever with all our scientific knowledge, yet in reality even in our scientific age we can only understand about 5% of the universe – the rest is dark energy or dark matter that is currently inaccessible to us.

The earth is not just a random lump of rock hurtling through space: God himself is its creator. It is exactly the size he meant it to be (v. 5). It is exactly where he meant it to be. Its mountains and valleys, its rain, hail and snow (vv. 22, 25–28, 37) are just as he intended. And these things matter: they are what make the earth a habitable planet. We can thank God for his wisdom in making such a wonderful home for us, one which God himself declared in the first chapter of Genesis to be 'very good'.

Guidelines

Ruth Bancewicz

This week's passages have focused on God's wisdom, providence and creative power. Everything was made for and through Christ, who is the embodiment of God's wisdom, and everything is sustained by him. God is sovereign over all creation, and he provides for every living thing. Try to set aside some time in the next couple of days to meditate on the implications of these truths by doing one of the activities below.

- Pick the study that spoke to you most clearly and spend a coffee break investigating one aspect of the science mentioned. Try to use reliable online sources, such as the NASA website, the Natural History Museum website or BBC science. Spend about half the time feeding your sense of wonder with the science, and the other half praising and thanking God, who created all these things.

- Choose one of the attributes of God that we have studied, writing down some words and phrases that help you to think about this aspect of his character and purposes in more detail – whether directly from the Bible or a summary in your own words of the biblical message. If you are feeling creative, you could try to shape these words and phrases into your own psalm.

- Find a new way of recognising and acknowledging your dependence on God, and see if you can build it into your regular daily or weekly routine. For example, can you include thanks for water and air into your daily prayers? What about thinking about where your food has been sourced and feeding that into your prayer if you say grace before a meal? How would you feel about regularly thanking God for the ultimate source of the power in your home, church or transport – whether it comes from fossil fuels or sustainable sources? Can you think of any other meaningful ways of remembering your dependence on God's provision and regularly expressing gratitude for it?

1 Everlasting

Hugh Rollinson

John 1:1–5

It can be hard to comprehend the idea of a 'beginning'. For many people the mountains have been there forever, although for me as a geologist, mountains are not permanent – they come and go through the vast cycles of time. A rather different but recent reminder of the very beginning was the Winchcombe meteorite, which fell out of the sky in February 2021 – this unspectacular rock was formed at the birth of our solar system some 4.57 billion years ago.

Our passage today reminds us that the Word was with God even before the beginning of time. William Barclay translates the opening sentence – 'When the world had its beginning, the Word was already there.'

So who or what was this mysterious Word? John cleverly uses the term *Logos* (literally in the Greek meaning word or reason) because it had a deep meaning for both the Jewish and Greek readers of his gospel and so had the power to connect with the two dominant cultural groups of his world.

For the reader of the Hebrew Bible, words had power. God's words were not simply there to convey information. Rather, they had a dynamic character and were designed to bring change, even to the point of bringing something that did not exist into being. This is particularly clear in the creation story of Genesis 1, strongly echoed in this passage. In later Judaism, as the name of God became particularly sacred, the term 'the word of God' became synonymous with the person of God himself. So, for the Jewish reader of John's gospel, the idea of the *Logos* represented the dynamic and creative power of God.

For the Greek convert to Christianity, the idea of the *Logos* had a different root and drew on the Greek philosophy of several centuries earlier. For Greek thinkers, the *Logos* was the power that made the world and which now sustained it. The *Logos* also represented that which made sense of the world. And so, to the Greek reader John is saying: since ancient times you have been trying to understand the power that made the world and the mind behind the universe; this *Logos* is now embodied in the person of Jesus who (incredibly) has lived among us.

2 Praiseworthy

Paul Ewart

Psalm 148

This psalm begins and ends with 'Hallelujah', an exhortation to praise God. Everything from the highest reaches of heaven to the smallest creatures on earth is called to praise its creator. Three questions arise. Why praise? How can inanimate objects or animals praise anyone? What is praise, anyway?

Two reasons for praise are suggested by the writer. The first (vv. 5–6), after the call upon everything in the heavens, recalls the opening chapter of Genesis, which declared that the sun, moon and stars were created by God, implying that they were not themselves deities to be worshipped, as was the practice of some religions. Written from the perspective of ancient cosmology, with waters above a solid dome or firmament, the poem nonetheless expresses the truth that the universe obeys law, i.e. the decree 'that will never pass away' (v. 6). The resulting regularity and order make possible the science that enhances our vision of the immensity of the universe. Coming down to earth, we see a diverse, interdependent creation, each living creature in its environment, the ecology revealed by our modern scientific perspective.

The second reason (vv. 13–14) reiterates that there is only one creator, who gives strength, a symbolic horn, to his people. He is not the remote deist god, the god of the philosophers, but the God of Abraham, Isaac and Jacob, concerned for every human from kings to women and children, before whom all are equal.

But how do stars, sea creatures or snowflakes praise God? Just by being what they are – showing power, life and beauty in splendid and wonderful variety. They not only show God's power and glory, as affirmed by Psalm 19:1–4 and Romans 1:20, but they are instruments in his hand and under his control, Luke 8:22–24. The inscription on the tomb of Sir Christopher Wren in St Paul's Cathedral, which he designed, reads, '*Si monumentum requiris circumspice.*' If you seek his memorial, look around you.

So, with vision enhanced also by science, seeing God in his artwork and action in creation, we see what praise is. Praise is not limited to singing complimentary songs about God or acknowledging his character; it is also what creation does simply by existing. If you want to see what praise is, look around you.

3 Powerful

Ruth Bancewicz

Luke 8:22–25

Some of Jesus' disciples had lived all their lives on the shores of Lake Galilee. Although they wouldn't have been able to explain the science behind it, they would have relied on their knowledge of the local weather in order to keep safe. We now know that it is the cold air sweeping down from nearby mountains that whips up sudden storms on this relatively enclosed and low-lying body of water. When Jesus invited the disciples to cross the lake, did a few of them murmur between themselves that the weather didn't look quite right for such a trip, or was the squall that suddenly blew in a surprise even to the seasoned sailors?

Luke seems to use the word 'Master' (rather than 'Teacher') when the disciples don't understand what Jesus is doing. The disciples were supposed to trust Jesus – but how? Did he expect them to calm the storm themselves, or was he disappointed that they were so amazed when he brought about calm? Did he mind that they asked for help in such a desperate way, or would he rather they just keep bailing and trust that they would be kept safe – as Jesus did while he slept? Most of commentators I consulted opted for one or other of the latter two options.

In the end, 'He who was sleeping was awakened and sent the sea into a sleep' (Ephrem the Syrian). Miracles don't have to defy science. In fact, knowing how something works can make a miracle all the more awe-inspiring. A meteorologist or sailor might be able to describe how a squall could leave as suddenly as it arrived, but that needn't explain away what Jesus did. The wonder was that the wind appeared to instantly obey Jesus' rebuke. The disciples might have seen a number of such 'coincidences' (or miracles of timing) by this point, but this one was the most surprising so far. With their knowledge of Galilean weather, they were well equipped to recognise Jesus' extraordinary authority over creation. What's more, they had just seen their teacher exercise the same power that they had learned, through scripture, is characteristic of the God of Israel. No wonder they were afraid!

4 Supreme

Robert White

Colossians 1:15–20

The scandal of the Christian gospel is that God himself became incarnate in Christ Jesus, became fully human. He was like us in every way except one: which is that he never sinned. Yet he wasn't just a messenger sent from heaven. He was fully God as well as fully man: all God's fullness dwelt in him (v. 19).

This passage tells us of the supremacy of Christ over the physical, material world we see around us; and also his supremacy over the spiritual world, the invisible world. His body was made of exactly the same kinds of atoms and molecules as our bodies. Yet more than that, those atoms and everything else were created through him and for him in the first place (v. 16). That is an astonishing thought. The very atoms of which our bodies are constructed were made in the furnace of stars under the sovereignty of Christ: yet isn't this fitting, that he used exactly that same material in his own body?

But Christ wasn't just a creator who made all of this incredible universe, and then left his masterpiece as a completed object. He also holds it in being continually (v. 17b). The picture is of him maintaining and sustaining the creation in all its consistency and order every minute of every day. For a scientist like myself, this is an incredible blessing he gives humanity. The very fact that we can do science, that the material world behaves consistently throughout space and time, that we live in a universe which is intelligible to our minds and so we can construct laws which describe how it works, is an immense gift from God. And so it behoves us to use that scientific understanding of the world for the good of humankind: that is part of how we worship God.

Christ is supreme not only over the material world, but also over the spiritual world. He is the head of the body of all believers, that is the church, and by his death on the cross he reconciled all things (v. 18): so believers can look forward not only to life in the eternal presence of God, with all sin banished, but to life in a renewed physical creation. Nothing in this world or the next is outside Christ's supremacy.

5 Knowable

Rodney Holder

Psalm 19 (NRSV)

The magnificence of the sky on a clear night is truly awesome and points to its creator. The creation makes God knowable, as the apostle Paul says explicitly in Romans 1:19–21. The message of the heavens is, however, wordless and 'their voice [Hebrew *qōl*] is not heard' (v. 3). Yet, paradoxically, 'their voice [Hebrew *qaw*] goes out through all the earth, and their words to the end of the world' (v. 4). Here *qaw* is more literally rendered 'line', which may carry the implication of 'measurement' and 'design'. But 'voice' (as in the Septuagint) also makes sense, since it is paralleled by 'words' in the second half of the sentence. The apostle Paul says that 'faith comes from what is heard, and what is heard comes through the word of Christ', but then, remarkably, cites Psalm 19:4 to say that they have heard of Christ through the creation (Romans 10:17–18)!

Does it matter that the cosmology of the passage is primitive? While we know the earth moves (but still speak of the sun rising and setting), in the psalmist's world view the earth was stationary. Moreover, we read that the 'firmament' proclaims God's handiwork. The Hebrew word *rāqia* means the metal dome or vault of heaven sitting over the earth in ancient cosmology, which Genesis 1:6 says was created on day two. For me, the theological message of the creation pointing to its creator becomes stronger the more we know about the universe, evoking even greater awe. For example, we now know that the sun is a very ordinary star, yet it is an 865,000-mile-diameter nuclear furnace radiating 400 trillion watts of power for billions of years. We also know that there are at least ten billion trillion stars in the observable part of the universe.

This psalm seamlessly moves from the heavens, and the movement of the sun, to the moral law, switching from 'El' for God to the covenant name 'Yahweh'. Immanuel Kant wrote: 'Two things fill the mind with ever new and increasing wonder and awe, the more often and the more seriously reflection concentrates upon them: the starry heaven above me and the moral law within me.'

6 Rest

Denis Alexander

Genesis 2:1–3

On the seventh day the work of creation is crowned and celebrated as 'God rested'. This powerful declaration of the completion of a good creation is for human benefit, as Exodus 20:8–11 makes clear. Regular rest is one of the great gifts of the Bible to humankind. In the Babylonian calendar of the ancient Near East, every seventh day was celebrated as an unlucky or 'evil day' on which certain activities were prohibited. On each of them offerings were made to a different god or goddess. But here in Genesis, the one creator God graciously bestows this gift of rest on humanity. Over the centuries, the 'gift of rest' has spread across the world, receiving a powerful impetus from Emperor Constantine, who officially adopted the seven-day week for the Roman empire in AD321, making Sunday a day of rest.

Jesus himself gave many wise insights as to how his followers should interpret the sabbath rest, retaining its principle while discarding oppressive interpretations. 'The sabbath was made for man,' he said, 'not man for the sabbath' (Mark 2:27). Lest people thought that healing on the sabbath was wrong, Jesus reminded them, 'My Father is always at his work to this very day, and I too am working' (John 5:17). Genesis 2:1–3 was not about God literally stopping his creative work – otherwise nothing would exist – but about us needing to take a good rest one day a week. Hyper-literalists in Jesus' day turned this wonderful guidance on how to exercise our freedom from over-work into a burdensome set of rules.

Today other hyper-literalists can turn the early chapters of Genesis into a discussion about science, when in fact such rich theological essays concern the realities of our daily personal lives. Ironically, some preachers and church leaders can give wonderful sermons on Genesis, but then suffer from burnout due to over-work. The writer to the Hebrews explains how deeply the sabbath rest should impact our lives, having implications not only for caring physically for our bodies, but also as a daily reminder that our dependence for salvation lies in faith not in works (Hebrews 4:10–11). The seventh day of creation continues to impact our lives, providing a profound release from salvation through works and from burdensome over-work.

Guidelines

Ruth Bancewicz

We have spent some of this week learning about all creation's praise and glorification of God, so why not try some outdoor worship at some point in the next few days? You could take these notes with you, focusing on the study that struck you most or helped you draw nearer to God. You might go alone, maybe stopping in a park on your walk to work, taking a break in the day to go for a walk outside or setting aside ten minutes to sit in the garden, if you have one. Alternatively you might choose to worship together – taking your family, church team or Bible study group outside to spend some time in a nearby green space. If it's very cold, you might prefer to adapt this activity for a brisk walk. If it's wet and you can't wait for the rain to stop, you might want to sit by a window (try to open it a bit if you can do so without the rain coming in too much).

- Take a few minutes to sit or stand still, taking in your surroundings with all of your senses.
- Read over the passage from your chosen study from the last week again, dwelling on any phrases that will help you – or the others with you – to worship God or meditate on an aspect of his character.
- Think about how the passage speaks to your surroundings as well as yourself, e.g. Colossians 1:17 speaks of all things holding together in Christ.
- Say some prayers of thanksgiving for the created world and God's relationship with it, or join in with the praise of creation around you in whatever way you feel comfortable.
- Before you go, how can you do some tending and keeping of the area you are in now? Can you pray about activities that affect it in negative or positive ways (e.g. nearby building or road works, greenhouse gas emissions, pollution), take some litter home for recycling, decide to include some care for the area as part of your regular church activities or plant some bee-friendly species?

FURTHER READING

Denis Alexander (ed.), *Has Science Killed God?* (SPCK, 2019).

Ruth Bancewicz, *Wonders of the Living World: Curiosity, awe and the meaning of life* (Lion, 2021).

Colin Bell and Robert White, *Creation Care and the Gospel: Reconsidering the mission of the church* (Hendrickson, 2016).

Peter Harrison, 'Religion and the rise of science', *Faraday Paper 21*, obtainable free from **faraday.cam.ac.uk** (click on 'Resources').

Rodney Holder, *Big Bang Big God: A universe designed for life?* (Lion 2013).

David Wilkinson, *The Message of Creation* (IVP, 2002).

Christian groups that focus on creation care: A Rocha UK (**arocha.org.uk**); Operation Noah (**operationnoah.org**); Tearfund (**tearfund.org**).

James

Rosalee Velloso Ewell

There is a saying, 'Every family is normal until you get to know it.' This applies even to Jesus' family! Imagine being the step-brother of the saviour of the universe, but only being persuaded of your relative's status sometime after his crucifixion and resurrection. This is what many scholars believe about the author of James – that he was the brother of Jesus, the same 'James the Just' that is mentioned as the leader of the church in Jerusalem in the book of Acts (e.g. Acts 15). While we know very little about the details of James' life, we have this letter, written with astonishing directness and boldness, challenging the church then and today to live lives worthy of faith in Jesus Christ.

Throughout Christian history there have been many questions raised about this letter, with some even attempting to dismiss it entirely from the Bible. As biblical scholar Elsa Tamez wrote, if the letter of James were sent to Christian communities today, it might be intercepted by government security agencies because of its subversive message and denouncement of the exploitation of peoples.

For James there is no dichotomy, no distinction between what one believes and what one does. Faith and works are intertwined wholly into one another so that the genuine believer and the real Christian community live out their faith visibly and truthfully in whatever context they find themselves.

James draws heavily on the teachings of Jesus and on Israel's scriptures. Indeed, it is difficult to read this letter without hearing the echoes of the Old Testament throughout its message. The author makes his case for righteous living in the world through vivid imagery (wilting flowers, fancy clothing, etc.) and strong language that cannot easily be brushed aside. Its prophetic words to followers of Christ then are just as powerful and relevant to followers today.

Unless otherwise stated, Bible quotations are from the NRSV. Author references are to works in the 'Further reading' list.

1 Looking for trouble

James 1:1–4

In some of the New Testament letters it seems necessary for the author to establish his authority and to use such status as part of the argument against false doctrines and unholy living. Paul, for example, typically starts his letters with 'Paul, an apostle of Christ Jesus…' (e.g. Galatians 1:1; 2 Corinthians 1:1). He does not do so arrogantly, but simply follows a typical format for an opening line. The template used by James is slightly different and sets the tone for the rest of the letter: followers of Christ are to be humble servants of this upside-down kingdom. James identifies himself not by his family ties to Jesus, but as a slave to God and to the Lord Jesus Christ.

At the time of the writing of this letter, probably around AD45, the Roman empire had its own form of globalisation. James' opening greeting to 'the twelve tribes in the Dispersion' (v. 1) reflects this reality. He writes to people living where they had not intended or desired to live, but were there by forced migration, persecution and displacement. How does one live faithfully under such difficult circumstances? James' answer comes in the form of an odd encouragement: be glad and look for trouble, because in such trials your faith will blossom and flourish.

At face value, James' words do not seem encouraging at all: 'Whenever you face trials of any kind, consider it nothing but joy' (v. 2). But these must be read in the context of James' own life and that vision of God's kingdom that he paints so vividly for his readers. He is not making light of trials and persecution. Rather, he is saying to those who might be feeling a bit down and discouraged about their lives – take heart! Jesus is your Lord and in him you are complete, even under pressure and persecution. Often the voices of evil and grim news are very loud. James is saying, 'Don't let them overwhelm you!' Even in difficult times, God is working in us and making us complete (v. 4) in ways we did not even know we were incomplete. My children talk about binge-watching a series because they are afraid of spoilers on social media. James is the spoiler here. He is reminding us of the final episode – that Christ will establish his kingdom – and that challenges today are preparing us for life with the God of love and justice.

2 Walking on thin ice

Have you ever considered what it would look like to superimpose two very different paintings? Imagine a huge painting of the sea and waves and a storm. Then add to that a portrait of a strange figure. Perhaps we are mixing Turners and Picassos. In these verses James is painting one such image. It is a mixture of wild nature and of a person disfigured by their lack of wisdom and understanding of God. When one lacks godly wisdom, one is walking on thin ice which will soon break and swallow you up. Yet despite the troubling image, there is hope. There is a promise – 'If any of you is lacking in wisdom, ask God, who gives to all generously and ungrudgingly' (v. 5).

These verses are about conviction and the things that drive us. Ask in faith without doubt, says James, and God is generous and will grant it to you. Again, this is about silencing those thunderous noises that lead us to question God's goodness. It is about recovering our hearing so that we can trust, really trust, in the God who raised Jesus from the dead. This is the God who gives wisdom, perseverance and faith to anyone who asks.

The element of trust is key in these verses. The one who doubts (v. 6) is like the foolish one – foolish because he can't discern between what is good and bad. There is a difference between foolishness and uncertainty. James knows that the people he is writing to are unsure of how things will work out and so he writes to reassure and to tell them, remember how the story ends and live accordingly. That which gives people security now, riches and wealth, is but temporary, so we must not place our trust in such things. With lively and perhaps disturbing pictures, James alludes to the image of Christ who was made low; he invites his readers to think about how fleeting is our worldly security. Finally, and perhaps most appropriate for our time, James highlights the dangers of 'a busy life' (v. 11) that actually distract us from the wisdom God is offering and from a life lived for Jesus. In line with his opening remarks, the author paints a picture of what a life lived under the lordship of Jesus looks like. Even in trials, this life of discipleship does not perish or wither under the scorching sun, but flourishes and is complete because of God's good, generous gifts.

3 What do you wish for?

James 1:12–17

When my children were little, they enjoyed retelling their dreams and often asked what I had dreamed of the night before. I could not remember, but I could tell them about daydreams. In this text James invites us to ask possibly embarrassing questions – what are your dreams about? What do you most desire? This is a text about what we long for and learning to have our wishes turned towards God alone. Ancient philosophers said, 'Tell me what you wish for and I will tell you who you are.' In these verses James is asking the same question – do you really desire God? If so, show me!

Using the imagery of a gladiator's battle and the crown of victory, James builds on the previous section to encourage his readers towards desiring God. Though they are lowly and dispersed, they have an unchanging, faithful and generous God (v. 17) who will never deceive them. In contrast to God's truth are our desires, which, when not turned towards God, become deceitful, harmful to ourselves and the community, and ultimately lead to death (v. 15).

Scholars debate James' sources and wonder how he could have known of Jesus' teachings. Whatever the answer to those debates, in this section there is an echo of Jesus' confrontation with Peter when Jesus says to him, 'Get behind me, Satan!' (see Matthew 16:22–24). In the gospel story, Peter does not want Jesus to suffer and so Jesus strongly rebukes him. Similarly here, James warns his readers about the temptation to avoid suffering and persecution , which leads us away from God, for we end up fearing death more than God. The desire to avoid suffering is enticing (v. 14), but it leads to sin and death.

The first fruits (v. 18) calls to mind the best of the crops, the choicest portions of meat that were set apart as offerings to God. Paul wrote that we should be thankful because God chose us as the first fruits of salvation (2 Thessalonians 2:13), and in this text James makes a similar argument. We have been birthed to life through God's truth, and it is this truth, not envy or evil wishes, that should shape how we live.

4 The word in action

This is perhaps one of the most well-known portions of James. Margaret Aymer (pp. 22–23) explains that in these few verses James lays out the three key themes that will dominate the rest of the letter. First, it is not anger or envy that will bring about God's justice, but patient endurance that is quick to listen and slow to speak (v. 19). Second, we are called to be doers of the word, and not merely hearers (v. 22). Third, there is a difference between true and false religion (vv. 26–27).

For James 'word' is not a noun, but a verb. It is active, and as it acts it can have harmful or beneficial results. Words are actions that change the course of history, that alter people's lives, their relationships and their communities. The word of God gives life, and it endures and overcomes the most challenging circumstances. In contrast, our words tend to be filled with anger, lies and envy, which only lead to death.

The Venerable Bede (c. 672–735) wrote concerning verse 19, 'It is stupid to think that someone who is not prepared to learn from others will somehow be well-equipped to preach to them.' Bede was writing to monks and pastors, but his admonition is equally valid for us. To be bearers of the good word of God is a process that requires learning and discernment. If we are not prepared to listen, we will remain stupid, as Bede says, and unable to be the disciples and witnesses of Christ we were created to be.

Tom Wright (p. 11) points out that in verse 21 James recalls the image from Isaiah 55 – the word implanted in us that has the power to save. Every Christian community needs to consider for itself what it looks like to be doers of the word of God, whether they are comfortably situated or suffering persecution.

Imagine not knowing what you look like. James argues that it is God's good law of liberty (v. 25) that can mirror to us our true image. God's law isn't a set of rules and regulations, but is concerned with justice, love and patience. The genuine disciple is the one who takes care of the widow and the orphan and the one who speaks words of love and peace. Discipleship is about embodying in heart, hands and mouth the word of God.

5 Doomed for taking sides

James 2:1–13

One of the outcomes of the Covid-19 pandemic has been to highlight the unequal access around the globe to healthcare, vaccines and basic human needs, such as good food and clean water. The world systems of economics and politics play favourites. And even when we protest about such inequalities or are grieved and pray in church for those less fortunate, we're not even close to grasping the severity of the matter as James argues in this text. Favouritism and taking sides are not just matters of justice or economics. They are matters of life and death. Showing signs of favouritism calls into question your very faith in Jesus (v. 1).

Perhaps James' readers are tempted to show favouritism in order to fit in, to be less oppressed or to have a little more control over their own destinies. But James' warnings are stark: if you take sides (especially the side of the rich) you have made yourselves judges with evil thoughts (v. 4). As Tamez points out (p. 21), for James the oppressors are the rich. He does not mince words or offer easy answers. As he has already said in 1:10–11, the rich will disappear like a flower in the field; they will wither away. Until they fade away, they are the ones responsible for the oppression of those who do good and therefore, God's people should never be on their side.

These were uncomfortable texts for James' readers, and they are uncomfortable for us today. With images and words that echo Jesus' sermon on the mount, James challenges all of us to consider very seriously what side we take. In 1:14 he had already talked about the things we wish for, and here he illustrates this vividly. Desiring riches places you on the side of the blasphemer and the oppressor. The alternative is to learn and to practise love of neighbour (vv. 8–9).

James recalls the image of the law of liberty (v. 12), which is the one that serves as a mirror for us. If we look carefully into this law, we are called to be merciful and kind, for according to such kindness and mercy will we also be judged. Kindness and mercy for James means being with the poor, it is the word of God active in us. When taking sides with the poor and the oppressed we will be blessed, for there also will we find our Lord.

6 What it takes to be God's friend

James 2:14–26

If we imagine that James was writing to mostly Jewish Christians scattered abroad, then we can assume that for these readers, the basic affirmations of faith in the one true God still stand: 'Hear O Israel, the Lord our God is One!' (Deuteronomy 6:4). This prayer, said in the mornings and evenings, would have helped shape and maintain the identity of the community in dispersion. James isn't challenging this prayer or this expression of worship of God. What he is saying is that if your words are not backed up by concrete actions that display the justice and love of this one God, then they are empty.

James' story of meeting a homeless and hungry person (vv. 15–16) evokes images that we encounter every day in the city centres of the world. Again, these are uncomfortable words because there is no middle ground, no grey area. You either back your words up with actions – food and clothing – or you fail in your faith. Puffed-up words, even if they are nice prayers, that are not put into action are indicators of a faith that is dead (v. 17).

The person who listens and learns the word of God (1:22–25) is the one who becomes a doer of the word rather than the senseless person. To strengthen his argument about the ways faith and works are intertwined, James calls to memory both Abraham and the prophet Isaiah. The story of Abraham's near-sacrifice of Isaac (Genesis 22) would have been familiar to James' readers. It was the point of ultimate testing of Abraham's faith. It is also the first time the word 'love' appears in the Bible (Genesis 22:2). We know how Abraham's story ends, but what James adds here is a reference to Isaiah 41 – that great affirmation that God is on the side of the oppressed people and will rescue them with God's mighty hand. In Isaiah 41:8 God calls Abraham 'my friend'. James' readers could easily identify with the people to whom Isaiah spoke – they too were in a foreign land, displaced and oppressed. Isaiah (and James) calls them to act faithfully, to work together, to show kindness and mercy to one another and so to be identified with Abraham, God's friend. James ends with Rahab, whose place in society might not be seen as worthy of God's kingdom, yet her protection of the spies (see Joshua 2) is counted as an example of faith in action.

Guidelines

The letter of James paints so many images and stories that could easily be situated in 21st-century life. Behind all these stories stands James' call to his readers to live lives worthy of the gospel of Christ, lives characterised by patience, love and justice. A question for us today is whether we have the ears to hear James asking the same of us. Among the key issues are:

- Persecution and displacement – we hear stories of Christians attacked and killed in other parts of the world and we wonder at their faith, courage and endurance. How does James challenge us to pray for them? What is the role of the Christian community in your area as it seeks to serve, to care for and to welcome migrants and refugees?

- Riches and busyness – James' words are difficult for all. In a world shaped by money and the desire for accumulation, the accusations of James that such desires are of the devil and lead only to death call into question the very comfortable lives for which we strive. And what would it look like in your context to practise patience as a way to mitigate against an ever-busier life?

- Words and actions – how do you behave when coming across a homeless person in your city centre? Are we more like the villagers in the story of Ruth who simply sat by watching the two poor widows arrive and did nothing to help them? How do the words of James challenge the church today to think about its responsibility for orphans or children in the care system?

1 Warning: words are a type of work

James 3:1–12

Developing the theme he began in 1:19 about the stupidity of the one who does not listen, here James applies it to all those who attempt to instruct others in the ways of the Lord. There was a certain distinction and status in being a teacher. The rabbis were teachers, as were the Pharisees. Many were good teachers. James is not criticising a class of people. His warning is for all because all of us are tempted at some time or another to think we have the right answers and that our way is the best. Such an attitude is not only prideful and arrogant, but it can also severely mislead others. Hence James says, 'We who teach will be judged with greater strictness' (v. 1).

Speaking truthfully and gently is part of practising one's faith. In chapter 2 the person who does not offer clothing and food to the naked and hungry is criticised not just for lacking in good works, but also for what they say with their tongue – 'Go in peace; keep warm and eat your fill' (2:16). What a horrible thing to say to one who is suffering! Our lack of faith is demonstrated also by the lies and empty promises we make.

James highlights with vivid examples the power that our speech has over our own bodies and over the community. A ship's rudder can lead it to safe harbours, but it can also lead it to crash among the rocks; a small spark can start a forest fire, even unintentionally. He points out the irony of using the same mouth both to bless God and to curse others whom God loves. 'Personal honesty, transparency among members of the community, is fundamental to praxis,' writes Tamez (p. 55). As we know from the many scandals in churches and the downfall of Christian leaders, deceitful speech tarnishes the whole body and deeply harms our witness of Christ to a watching world.

Truthful speech and acts of justice are intimately tied together. James has already written that we are born of the word of truth and we are the fruits of God's creation (1:18). He ends this section again with the image of fruits, showing how we cannot bless God with our tongue and then act unjustly towards other people (v. 9). By our good fruit – by our truthful speech and generous works – we display our faith in God as individuals and as a community of Christ.

2 Being a 'glass-half-full' disciple

We have seen that works and faith are intertwined, along with words and our speech. Behind these or even as their source, James adds our thoughts and outlook on life and the world around us and calls his readers to be disciples of Christ whose outlook is that 'the glass is half full'. Yes, there are challenges and evil in the world, but we know the end of the story and so our lives, our actions, our talk and our perspectives ought to reflect this knowledge of the goodness, justice and peace of God.

God gives true wisdom to whoever asks honestly (1:5–6). With such wisdom we are enabled to see the world and one another with eyes of compassion and love. These stand in contrast to the unwise, who are filled with bitterness and envy (v. 14). We must show our faith through our good life (v. 13). In a world of fake news and social media it is easy to be cynical and to allow cynicism and harsh words to dominate our outlook on life and the world. James' warnings are harsh – that sort of wisdom, that sort of worldview, is from the devil (v. 15).

These verses describe the character of our life together. What do you desire most? Are such desires all about you? If so, then these will lead to disorder and 'wickedness of every kind' (v. 16). The true follower of Christ is the one marked by gentleness, mercy and peace (v. 17). Jesus' words in the sermon on the mount echo in these verses: 'Blessed are the peacemakers, for they will be called children of God' (Matthew 5:9).

For James' readers and for us, there is always the temptation to seek status and power to overcome whatever challenges we might be facing. The subversive message of the gospel, however, is that challenges and temptations are overcome through suffering, mercy and a 'harvest of justice' that leads to peace (v. 18).

3 Living together

We return once more to the theme of friendship with God, but this time we are not told of Abraham or Rahab. Rather, James examines friendship from its opposite, enmity, and asks two questions: first, what leads us to be enemies of God? And second, what can we do to overcome this tragic situation? The answer to both questions has to do with how we live together. As Luke Timothy Johnson explains (p. 187), the structure of this passage is complex, but it seems clear the author is setting up a conversation. There is the accuser, who offers the indictment of how things have gone wrong, and there is the defence on how to set it all right again.

To be friends with the world (v. 4) means putting my own desires and wishes ahead of everyone else's and ahead of what God asks of me. It means falling into the trap of trying to secure my own wealth and status rather than seeking the humility and acts of mercy to which God has called me. As Wright puts it in reference to verse 2, 'My cause is so important it's worth fighting and killing for' (p. 28).

James has already told his readers that God gives his children good gifts (1:5), but the condition for such gifts is honesty, truthfulness and humility on our part. It is not possible to try to fit into the club called 'world' and also be part of God's family. As Jesus put it, you cannot serve two masters (Matthew 6:24).

The path to recovery comes in the form of confession and repentance (vv. 7–10). We must learn to be friends with God by recognising our errors, lamenting for the many mistakes we have made and submitting to God. Typical of James, these are not things to do 'in theory'. Having our world view, our thoughts and our actions directed towards Christ are all works (signs) of our faith. It is about speaking well of one another and not gossiping. Imagine a Christian community known for its gracious and truthful speech. What a beautiful picture! James ends this section with the warning: if you cannot be such a community of grace, humility and love, in words and deeds, then you have placed yourselves in the role of judge, and for this you yourselves will be judged harshly.

4 A grim picture of power and wealth

In written Spanish, the text gives the reader a warning when a question or an exclamation is coming up with the upside-down symbols of either a question mark (¿) or an exclamation point (¡). James does something similar in these two sections, like the ringing of an alarm clock to wake his readers up from their laziness. Attention! Come now! Listen carefully, you talkers and you rich people (4:13; 5:1). These were uncomfortable texts for the people then and they certainly push us to the edge of our comfort zones now because these are subversive words that paint grim pictures of what it looks like outside the kingdom of God.

In the first picture James addresses those who talk and make plans about life without any reference to God. Much like the people in the tower of Babel (Genesis 11), they go about their daily lives, building the tower, planning their own greatness and securing their fame without consulting God or even considering that actually their lives are in God's hands. They boast in arrogance, and such boasting is evil (4:16). Though they have not taken notice of God, God has noticed them.

The second picture is of different types of skeletons. There are the rusted bones (dust) of what once were treasures of gold and silver, the rags that once were elegant robes and the bones of the rich themselves, their flesh eaten like fire (5:3). This sombre, terrifying image includes the murdered bodies of the oppressed and creation laid waste because of the pleasures of the rich (5:5).

As scattered and oppressed communities of the faithful, James' readers might have been tempted often to try to secure power and wealth to get themselves out of their dire situation. But as we have seen in 1:27, 2:6–7 and elsewhere in this letter, to be on the side of the rich and the oppressor means being on the side of evil and death. James does not want this for his readers (or for us!). So he reminds them that God's kingdom is subversive, exposing the reality that riches and power are mere skeletons.

5 Learning to be like Job

James 5:7–12

In contrast to the bleak paintings of the previous section, James here draws an almost impressionistic landscape of fields well-watered, using the story of the patient farmer to urge his readers to persevere. His harsh references to the judgement and death that come to the rich and powerful are plainly given because he loves the communities to which he writes. As beloved sisters and brothers, they must not fall into the traps of worldly desires or the impatience of taking matters into their own hands.

Patience and endurance return as major themes. Here they stand as the means by which we learn to place our hope and trust God. Wright explains (pp. 37–38) that every generation of Christians must learn anew what it means to wait for Christ's return and must recall that God's timing is not the same as ours, hence patience is a virtue that the Spirit gives us.

The ever-practical James spells out once more some of the characteristics of such patience, namely, watching how one speaks to another person: 'Do not grumble against one another, so that you may not be judged' (v. 9). Patience and endurance strengthen one's faith and are reflected in words and actions of truth and justice. As examples of these, James mentions the prophets (v. 10) and Job (v. 11). The prophets are the ones who brought the word of God to the people, even when those people did not want to hear or obey God's word. Job's endurance of suffering was characterised by his truthful speech (think of the ways he answered his friends) and by the vision of God's just reign – a kingdom precisely shaped by what James calls 'true religion' (compare 1:27).

Verse 12 is another example that scholars use to show the parallels between the letter of James and Jesus' teachings. Was James there when Jesus preached that famous sermon? Who knows! What matters for James and for his readers is that they learn to live consistent with the character, words and deeds of Jesus. Though they may be exiled and oppressed, their praise of God (speech) and their love of neighbour, enemy or even of oppressor (works) must always go hand in hand.

6 Communities of prayer and mercy

James closes his letter not with the traditional greetings we are accustomed to in letters such as Paul's. He does not name individuals, but refers again to his readers as 'brothers and sisters' (v. 19). Johnson writes:

James is communitarian… [he] calls on individuals only insofar as their single-mindedness is required to build and support the ethos of the community… James sketches a community whose speech and action express such collaboration and solidarity, nowhere more powerfully than in the gathering of the church in response to… its weakest members (p. 234).

Prayer for James is not wishful thinking or self-delusion, but a practice that demonstrates our faith in God and the fact that our lives exist within God's great story. A community shaped by prayer, mercy and acts of peace-making is one that looks out for its weakest members. This is the community characterised by true religion, and so it cares for widows and orphans (1:27).

God has equipped the church with the gifts of prayer and anointing with oil, and James has already told us the importance of confession and humility for the health of the community (4:8–10). As Wright explains:

James seems, again like Jesus himself, to have seen a connection between sin and ill-health… Maybe these are the two things that push to the fore when we take our stand in the place where prayer makes sense, at the place where heaven and earth overlap, and at the place where our present time and God's future time overlap (p. 42).

God's time is not our time, which means that patience is again highlighted as one of the key practices of a godly community. With patience and humility we must strive to keep one another practising the faith we have in Christ and not let anyone drift away (v. 19).

Waiting for the Lord is not easy. Through images and stories of patient farmers and practices of love and justice made possible because God is near to us (4:8) and forgives our sins (v. 15), James calls his readers to live anew in God's kingdom. Imagine what it is like to be part of a community where God is so near! It is transformative, shining like stars even in the darkest night. Love, prayer, compassion and peacemaking are the stars of faithful works.

Guidelines

- In a world shaped by social media, the rise of influencers and so many striving after status and fame, it is difficult and challenging to hear James' call to humility and suffering. What would it look like today for church leaders not to be famous or important? How can the Christian community learn to be a place where the weakest and lowliest person is the one who displays the marks of Jesus?

- Words are dangerous. Consider the waves of changing politics over the past years, the angry shouting even between Christians who disagree on social issues, economics or the right and wrong of a vaccine. To learn to listen to others and to God's Spirit takes practice. Learning not to talk takes even more practice. How can churches or even families be places where we practise listening and silence in order to hear God's loving voice?

- Patience emerges as a major theme throughout the letter of James. In a culture that gets anxious even with a small traffic jam, what would it look like to slow our lives down, to be patient enough to talk to the person on the street or the neighbour with whom we don't even get along and to learn their story? This is what James asks his readers and us to do – to be doers of God's word means waiting and practising a type of love that the world does not know, and so to show the world the love of Christ.

FURTHER READING

Margaret Aymer, *James: Diaspora rhetoric of a friend of God* (T&T Clark, 2017).

Luke Timothy Johnson, *Brother of Jesus, Friend of God: Studies in the letter of James* (William B. Eerdmans, 2004).

Elsa Tamez, *The Scandalous Message of James: Faith without works is dead* (Crossroad Publishing Company, 2002).

Tom Wright, *Early Christian Letters for Everyone: James, Peter, John and Judah* (SPCK, 2011).

2 Thessalonians

Steve Walton

Paul, Silvanus and Timothy had planted the church in Thessalonica (Acts 17:1–10) but were forced to leave the city after a short time (perhaps something over three weeks, Acts 17:2). Their first letter included teaching about the Lord's return, something they hadn't been able to teach fully about during their short visit (1 Thessalonians 1:10; 4:13—5:11), as well as mentioning the persecution the new believers faced (1 Thessalonians 2:14–16). The second letter is written not long after the first, maybe as little as a few weeks, because the situation has deteriorated. The church faces three major challenges which this letter addresses – look for these as we read the letter together.

First, the suffering and persecution has stepped up a gear, and probably caused some of the believers to wobble in their faithfulness to Jesus. The missionaries stress the deliverance which will come to believers at the Lord's return and the judgement which their opponents will face, and they encourage them to focus on Jesus as the source of their hope (1:4–12; 2:16–17; 3:3–4).

Second, there are misunderstandings about the day of the Lord's return, with some thinking that day has already arrived (2:2). Some may have misunderstood the first letter's teaching on that theme, and/or other teachers may have introduced strange ideas into the church. The team write to clarify the situation (2:1–15).

Third, a group within the church are being disruptive and refusing to work (3:6–15). They are depending on others' goodwill and resources to live, and this is causing tensions within the church. The missionary trio write their toughest words in responding to this issue.

It's worth reading the whole letter at a sitting as you start, to get an overview – that should take you 10–15 minutes. Unless otherwise stated, scripture quotations are taken from the NRSV.

1 Greetings, grace and peace

2 Thessalonians 1:1–2

As usual in ancient letters, we begin with the senders – Paul, Silvanus (sometimes called Silas) and Timothy – and the recipients – the church of the Thessalonians. Paul's team planted the church in Thessalonica (Acts 17:1–10) and have written earlier the letter we know as 1 Thessalonians. They are writing again in very similar terms to the opening of their previous letter (1 Thessalonians 1:1), which implies that they are still together. That places this letter soon after the first one, perhaps by only a matter of weeks. Much of this letter will sound familiar to readers of the first letter: it seems issues among the Christians in the city which the missionaries wrote about in the previous letter have developed – not to say gone pear-shaped – and now need further response.

Two things are striking as small differences from the greeting in 1 Thessalonians. First, they write of 'God *our* Father' (v. 1), whereas the previous letter spoke of 'God *the* Father'. Like the previous letter, this one is full of family language for the Christians (e.g. 'brothers and sisters', 1:3), and thus 'our' stresses that God has drawn them into his family through the Lord Jesus – and in that way they are different from other groups which used family language about each other, such as the Greek trade associations. The primary relationship they have is that they are now located *in* God and the Lord Jesus. That's crucial in their present situation, where they are suffering for their faith – understanding that they are safe in God's hands and belong to Jesus together is vital.

Second, the senders specify the source of the grace and peace they pray for as the same God (this time, *the* Father) and the Lord Jesus Messiah (v. 2). As often in other Pauline letters, the opening hints at themes which will return during the letter. The generosity of God – his grace – is the source of 'eternal encouragement and good hope' (2:16). God's generous love means the believers can face the challenges of their time, including suffering and death, with confidence. The peace of God is relevant amid persecution, too. It will keep them stable when their circumstances might make them wobble in their faith, and so the closing of the letter returns to this theme by praying again that the Lord, who is the source and meaning of peace, will give them peace (3:17).

2 Thanksgiving in trials

It's easy to think of the Thessalonian Christians feeling discouraged in the persecution they were facing (v. 4). They faced opposition, which probably included social isolation and exclusion, verbal harassment and attacks, and maybe physical abuse. This was true when the missionaries sent their first letter (e.g. 1 Thessalonians 2:14; 3:2–5), and Timothy's report had reassured them that the believers were standing firm in their faith (1 Thessalonians 3:6–8). By the time of this second letter, things have certainly not improved, and the believers would have felt a strong sense of social dishonour in their culture.

It is striking, therefore, that Paul's team are thankful for these relatively new Christians, and even boast about them to other churches. The team feel obligated to give thanks (v. 3), and saying that would prompt the Thessalonian believers to recognise that they were obligated to be thankful to God too.

In giving thanks to God for the believers, the missionaries bring encouragement as they lift the eyes of the church to God. They are thankful for two main things: the growth of their faithfulness to Christ, and the growth of their love for one another (v. 3). 'Faith' here is not simply an inner attitude of trust, but primarily active faithfulness or loyalty to Christ – 'steadfastness and faith' (v. 4) means 'steadfastness in faith'. They are hanging on in there, continuing to trust Jesus and to live for him amid suffering.

Not only that, but the evidence is visible in their love for one another. This is a committed mutual love of the whole community; the authors pile up phrases to show this: 'the love of *every one of you for one another*'. Churches can disintegrate into cliques at times, but not in Thessalonica at this time. External pressure brought them together in mutual encouragement and love. This love needed to be deeply practical, offering hospitality, sharing food and providing work for each other, because others in the city were turning their backs on the believers.

So, when Paul's team boasts about the Thessalonian believers, it's concerning their persistent faithfulness amid suffering. These Christians were models of following Jesus, from whom others could learn and take encouragement (see 1 Thessalonians 1:6–8). Suffering for Christ is not easy – but when other Christians learn that believers are staying faithful in persecution, it's a great encouragement.

3 Judgement for good or ill

2 Thessalonians 1:5–10

The Thessalonian Christians face tough times in suffering for their faith in Jesus (v. 5), and the writers address this issue directly. The team's response is rooted in who God is and how God acts: the God whom the believers know in Jesus Christ is just and acts rightly. This has consequences for both the believers and their persecutors, which they state briefly in verses 6–7a and then fill out in verses 7b–10.

When we hear 'judgement', we tend to hear it negatively, focusing on the condemnation and punishment of those found guilty. However, judgement has two sides: one party is found innocent and goes free, and the other party is found guilty and faces punishment. When the writers mention 'the righteous judgement of God' (v. 5), they are talking about both sides of the judgement coin.

The believers can be confident that their suffering is not the act of a capricious God who doesn't really love them. Rather, their persecution is time-limited and can have positive outcomes. The time limit is the return of Jesus (vv. 7, 10), and on that great day they will experience 'relief' (v. 7) – their suffering will be over – and they will be swept up into marvelling at Christ as they meet him face to face (v. 10). The authors hammer the point home: 'This includes you' (v. 10, NIV) because the Thessalonians believed the missionaries' testimony about Jesus. Knowing this helps make their suffering bearable, as well as helping them to understand that their suffering is training, preparing them for God's kingdom by shaping them into the people Jesus is making them to be (v. 5).

Their opponents will face the other side of God's judgement, which the missionaries characterise as eternal separation from the Lord (v. 9, echoing Isaiah 2:10). The great tragedy for people who reject ('do not obey') the gospel of Jesus and thus do not know God (v. 8) is that God lets them go and does not force them to respond. If you hate God and his people here and now, then why would you want to spend eternity with them? Incredibly sadly, such people miss out on all that makes people most human, living with God and his people. This motivates Paul and his team to announce the gospel as widely as possible while they can.

4 Praying in pain

2 Thessalonians 1:11–12

As I write, Afghanistan has been taken over by the Taliban, and there are stories that they are making threats to underground Christian groups in the country. Christians elsewhere are rightly being called to pray for our brothers and sisters in that land: but how should we pray in the face of such a threat? We learn about praying for suffering believers from these verses, as Paul's team turn their encouragement (vv. 5–10) into prayer. It's worth noticing what they *don't* pray for as well as what they do pray for.

My tendency, as a westerner, is to think that suffering is a bad thing – in wealthier countries, we have healthcare systems designed to avoid pain and suffering. For us as Christians, that can easily become the expectation that God will make our lives better and easier, that the Lord will remove pain from us. It's striking, then, that this is not what the missionaries pray for the Thessalonians – they don't ask God to deliver them from the suffering they're experiencing. Indeed, the writers consider suffering to be a part of the normal Christian life: remember how verses 3–5 show that suffering generates perseverance and faith.

Instead, the missionaries' prayer is twofold, linking back to the encouragement of verses 5–10. First, they pray that God will enable them to live in a way which matches up to God's call on their lives, that their profession of faith and lifestyle may be in tune. Second, they pray that God will empower them to live out their desires for goodness and cause it to grow (notice the fruit image). They're praying for the believers *in* the situation of pain and suffering, not asking for them to be removed from that situation. Why? Because that's how Jesus will be glorified, that's how his reputation will sparkle among their fellow citizens. Persistent faith in suffering has that kind of quality and effect on others around. Not only that, but Jesus' glory will be reflected back to them, as they persist in their faith through to the end of all things, when they will meet the Lord face to face (see vv. 7, 10). Here's a great way to pray for Christians who suffer for their faith today.

5 A strange letter and a reply

2 Thessalonians 2:1–6

The second coming of Jesus to judge and transform the world was central to the initial evangelism of Thessalonica (see 1 Thessalonians 1:10). That teaching led to questions which the missionary team answered in their first letter (1 Thessalonians 4:13—5:11). They now return to this theme (v. 1), which suggests that further questions and issues has arisen in the church. Specifically, the believers are concerned about a letter claiming Paul's authority to tell them that the day of the Lord has already arrived – the age to come is already in progress (v. 2). To our ears, this sounds strange, for we think of the Lord's coming as the time when everyone will see him and will bow to Jesus as Lord. However, these relatively new Christians aren't sufficiently established to know this for sure, and thus easily misled. They may have been told, worryingly, that their suffering is part of the judgement which the day of the Lord brought, or they may have misunderstood the teaching in the previous letter.

There's plenty to puzzle over in this section, but the central thing to notice is that the writers are saying clearly that there are more events to come before the great day of the Lord, just as they said in their first letter. That day definitely isn't here in its fullness yet. The missionaries are not saying anything they haven't already said (v. 5). They're not laying out a timetable of those events, but they are saying that things will get worse, not better, before the day comes.

There will be a 'lawless one' (v. 3) who will seek worship for himself (v. 4), and Paul has warned them about this (v. 5). Much Christian ink has been spilled in trying to guess this person's identity: perhaps he's an archetypal figure who can be seen in many individuals down the ages who have sought worship and ultimate allegiance for themselves in place of the true God (v. 4). For the Thessalonians, the Roman emperor demanded the loyalty and worship which the missionaries taught belonged to Jesus alone. The key point the writers stress is that this 'lawless one' will not triumph: he is 'destined for destruction' (v. 3). He's being restrained (v. 6), perhaps by the archangel Michael, who holds back evil and protects God's people in Daniel 10—12. They write to comfort and encourage, not to invite speculation – the Thessalonian Christians truly are safe in Jesus' hands.

6 Encouragement in tough times

2 Thessalonians 2:7–12

It's important to keep the senders' aim in focus here: they write to encourage the Thessalonians amid suffering for their faith. They aren't offering them a timetable of events to come at the end of all things. They're reminding the believers of things they have already taught them (v. 5) – and that can leave us puzzled, since we didn't hear that teaching. That's why we need to give attention as readers to the main point the writers are making.

The team remind the Thessalonian Christians that things are already difficult (v. 7), but events haven't yet reached their climax (v. 8). When that climax comes, Jesus will triumph and those who reject him will face judgement and loss (vv. 8–12). How does this teaching support and encourage the believers in tough times?

First, it helps them to see that, although things are bad, they could be much worse, because the restrainer holds back the full power of the 'lawless one' (vv. 6–7). They aren't facing the full force of evil because God, through this restrainer, is holding evil back, and for that they can be thankful.

Second, they can look forward with hope to the coming of Jesus, for he will literally blow the 'lawless one' away (v. 8). The image comes from Isaiah, where the Lord will judge justly for the needy and 'with the breath of his lips he shall kill the wicked' (11:4; see also 30:33). There's no battle here – there is no threat that Jesus will lose, or even be under pressure, in bringing justice and judgement. The believers can rejoice and can look their present experience of suffering in the eye without fear, for they can be confident of their ultimate vindication and safety (see also 1:1:6–10).

Third, the missionaries remind the believers that what they believe is the truth which brings them salvation (vv. 10, 12). To reject that good news is to reject life and to give in to wickedness and live a lie (v. 9). Sin is an addiction: the more you get into it, the more you want to get into it – remember the way that Paul three times speaks of God giving sinful people up to go their own way (Romans 1:24, 26, 28). *But that isn't the way the believers' lives are orientated* – that's the key point. The readers can take comfort from their safety in Christ.

Guidelines

The Thessalonian believers are having a hard time maintaining their faithfulness to Jesus because of opposition and disinformation. The opposition probably means that they find it hard to get work, lose customers from their shops and businesses, suffer social ostracism and perhaps are physically attacked. In the history of the church, persecution is not unusual – it is the normal situation for many believers today, who experience many of the same deprivations as the Thessalonians, plus being excluded from education which could help them out of poverty and struggle.

The striking thing with such believers is how often they are remarkably joyful and vibrant in their faith. They experience the Lord's grace and peace. They look forward to the day of Jesus' return when he will put the universe to rights. That's not to romanticise persecution at all: these Christians really do suffer, sometimes grievously, but they face it with the Lord standing by them. Polycarp, a second-century bishop of Smyrna, was put to death because he refused to deny his faith. He said to the magistrate, 'For eighty-six years I have been [Christ's] servant, and he has done me no wrong. How can I blaspheme my King who saved me?' (*Martyrdom of Polycarp* 9:3). He was so grateful to Jesus that he considered it no loss to die.

It's easy for us who live in comfortable places, where our faith is not a direct cause of persecution, to slip into mediocrity in our Christian lives. We can easily forget that this world is not as God wishes, that the day will come when the Lord Jesus judges everyone, and that we're called to live here as witnesses to Jesus. The letter of 2 Thessalonians calls us to reflect and to grasp that our Lord and Saviour is the most important one in the universe – he deserves our total allegiance.

1 Reasons for thanksgiving and confidence

2 Thessalonians 2:13–15

Paul, Silvanus and Timothy have reminded the Thessalonian believers of the truth about the day of the Lord (vv. 1–12), and now turn to response. The missionaries pray for Christians: verses 13–14 focus on thanksgiving, and verses 16–17 on intercession. Turning the truth into prayer is vital – as you read the Bible, think: is there something here to give thanks or praise God for, to ask or confess?

Paul's team are grateful for God's love for and God's choice of the Thessalonians (v. 13), language which echoes God's love and choice of Israel in scripture (e.g. Deuteronomy 7:7–10). Here's a basis for confidence – they were brought into God's people and God doesn't give up on his own.

They are the 'first fruits' of salvation (v. 13) – the first to trust in Jesus in their city. Here's another scriptural image, of the offering the Israelites brought to the Lord from the first produce from their fields (e.g. Deuteronomy 26:1–16). The image points to more fruit to come – more believers will be added to their church as God works.

They experience these wonderful things through God's work by the Spirit in combination with their trust in the truth they learned (v. 13). God works in their lives as they walk in faith, trusting that even when things appear dark – as they do now, in persecution – God has not abandoned them.

At the end of their Christian journey, the believers can be confident of 'the glory of our Lord Jesus Christ' (v. 14). The last word does not go to suffering and shame, for they will experience total renewal in the world to come when they see Jesus face to face. They will have 'relief' (1:7) and will marvel at Jesus on that day (1:10).

This thanksgiving is the basis of the encouragement to 'stand firm' in their faith and to 'hold fast' to the teaching they have received (v. 15). Rather than being 'shaken in mind or alarmed' (2:2), knowing the truth they were taught will set them free to keep going in the Christian walk. When life is dark and puzzling, when believers are suffering, they are to look afresh at the great truths of God's love, choice and power, and through them the Spirit will enable them to keep going.

2 Praying for progress

Here's part 2 of the missionaries' prayer for the believers, turning from thanks to intercession. They pray the content of the thanksgiving (vv. 13–14) into the Christians' lives. The God to whom they pray is the God who loves and gives generously (v. 16, echoing v. 13).

This being one of the earliest Pauline letters, it is striking that the missionaries pray to both Jesus and the Father here (v. 16) and have already spoken of the Spirit as the one who makes believers holy (v. 13). They pray naturally to Jesus – a stunning thing for Jewish people to do, for their whole upbringing told them to pray to God alone. Yet within a short time after Jesus' death and resurrection (perhaps 18 years), they recognise Jesus as an appropriate recipient of prayer. The devotion the missionaries offer Jesus marks him out: he reigns alongside the Father and acts in concert with the Father in answering prayer.

This God, known as Father and Son, gives 'encouragement' (v. 16, NIV), perhaps a better translation than the NRSV's 'comfort', which could sound like they are just saying, 'There, there.' Rather, God comes alongside them to strengthen them, and this happens in their 'hearts' (v. 17). We moderns think of the heart as the place of the emotions, but for ancient people it was the place of the will and decision-making. So the team pray for that encouragement to sink deep into their wills and lives, enabling them to 'stand firm' (v. 15) in a tough situation.

Paul's team pray for the wills and lives of the Thessalonians to head in the right direction, a direction which will produce 'every good work and word' (v. 17). A good life means a life which is fruitful for God's kingdom, a life which displays God's love, grace and power to those who meet it. They echo the prayer of 1:11, which asks God to 'bring to fruition' (NIV) their resolve to live with Jesus as Lord, to produce lives prompted by their trust in him. This something the missionaries pray for not just once, but repeatedly, even within one letter, because it's vital that the Christian hope for the future (v. 16) is displayed in the present, in the lifestyles of the believers. That's how they will bring glory to Jesus in their own transformed lives and in the impact their testimony to Jesus has among their fellow Thessalonians.

3 Pray for us!

Paul is not a proud man, unwilling to share his concerns and weakness with others. He and his team ask the Thessalonian Christians to pray for them (vv. 1–2). The missionaries know that they are reliant on God's power and grace for their ministry and lives, just as the Thessalonians are. As the team have prayed for the Thessalonians (2:13–17), they now seek the believers' prayers for the gospel to continue to spread, and for them to be rescued from 'wicked and evil people', which is probably a reference to opponents of the missionaries. If the team are writing from Corinth, then that fits with the threat they experience there from the Jewish synagogue, who throw Paul out and seek to persuade the provincial authorities to imprison him (Acts 18:5–17). Missionaries are not super-Christians, immune from pressure and opposition, but fallible humans who feel the opposition they face. The prayer request here shows us ways to pray for cross-cultural missionaries today.

You can almost see the wheels turning in the authors' minds as they recall that the Thessalonian believers are facing similar pressures, and so they encourage the recipients again that the Lord is entirely trustworthy and will keep them safe from all that Satan ('the evil one', v. 3) throws at them. The missionaries are confident in the faithfulness and persistence of the believers because they 'have confidence in the Lord' – trusting Jesus and trusting his people go together here (v. 4).

This confidence leads the team to pray for the believers again (v. 5), this time asking the Lord to keep them focused on God's love for them in Jesus, seen in the way Jesus stayed his course and can thus enable them to stay their course. This is what seeing the Lord's word spreading and being glorified (v. 1) looks like on the ground: lives which are full of God's love and which draw deeply on God's strength to keep going. The authors want the believers' attention to be on the Lord, whose love has drawn them to himself and who will sustain them, without ignoring the opposition they face. The writers speak plainly about that opposition here and elsewhere in the letter – but they want the believers' hearts to attend most closely to the Lord, who loves and empowers them, and they pray to that end.

4 Dealing with the disrupters (1)

Paul's team turn to a key issue: there are a group of believers in Thessalonica causing problems. The writers have sought first to direct the believers to Christ; now they address this concern in the light of their repeated call to focus on Jesus. They do this at some length (verses 5–15 speak about them), which suggests this is a serious problem.

What's the issue? They say these people are 'idle' (vv. 6, 11, NIV) – or perhaps we should translate that as 'disorderly' or 'rebellious'. They are doing the wrong things, not doing nothing: they are 'busybodies' (v. 11). This could mean two things, or perhaps a combination of them. First, they may be dependent as clients of wealthier people, supported financially and physically by these patrons (as they were called). Such relationships could be unhealthy, particularly if the patron was not a believer, for the client was required to support the patron's concerns and causes in order to keep the patron's help and resources coming. Second, the disruptive people may be claiming leadership in the church and expecting to be free from earning a living to do that. They were busy about what they thought was the Lord's work, but in fact they were sponging off church members, particularly wealthier ones.

The missionaries contrast the disrupters' lifestyle with their own example: they worked hard in order not to be dependent on the believers (vv. 7–8; see 1 Thessalonians 2:9). The model of the Christian life they offered was a working life (v. 9), so that the believers would imitate such financial independence. If Christians worked, they would not be dependent on a patron's whims. If they worked, they would not burden other believers by demanding financial support. It seems that the team taught the believers about this when they were in the city (v. 6), and they were now reminding them of it.

Given that most believers in the first century were poor or relatively poor, such teaching is challenging – if a believer gave to another, that was something not available to their own family. Yet such support is an example of the way Christ puts people back together to be givers and not only takers. To have work would mean that, like the missionaries, they could support others, even from small resources – for love for fellow believers, and for non-believers, is a key priority (see 1 Thessalonians 4:9–12).

5 Dealing with the disrupters (2)

What to do when some believers are acting wrongly, causing internal problems and giving the church a bad name among outsiders? Having identified the problem (vv. 6–9), Paul, Silvanus and Timothy now address how the believers should respond to the disrupters in their community and speak directly to these people.

The team remind both groups of a key piece of teaching (v. 10). It's worth reading verse 10 twice to see what it says: it isn't saying that a person who *does not* work should not eat, but that a person who is *unwilling* to work should not eat. The issue isn't opportunity, but desire. They certainly want believers to help fellow Christians who *cannot* work because of family circumstances or disability or illness (v. 13). But the missionaries warn against people who refuse to work, for such people cannot be part of the body of Christ's care for others.

The missionaries characterise the disrupters as 'busybodies' (v. 11), a word found elsewhere in the New Testament only in 1 Timothy 5:13. There, the busybodies wander from house to house gossiping. The missionaries call them to change their ways: to earn the money to buy food (v. 12), rather than sponging off others. Godliness is not an excuse for laziness!

The team calls the other believers to continue doing the right things (v. 13), working hard and supporting others as much as they are able. If the disrupters persist in their sponging, they are to shame them by dissociating from them (v. 14), a powerful action in a society where honour and shame were key values. Being publicly shamed was one of the worst things a person or a family could experience.

However, the believers are not to reject them entirely, but are to seek to win them back by warning them earnestly – and that may be part of what keeping doing the right thing means (v. 13). They are not to cut them off finally and forever, but to call on the disrupters to mend their ways (v. 15). There's a fine balance here between warning and rejecting, but it's vital to know the difference and to be prepared to have a tough conversation with a fellow believer who is acting wrongly, especially if they are giving the Lord and his people a bad reputation as a result.

6 Wrapping up

Paul, Silvanus and Timothy close their letter with two prayers (vv. 16, 18) and an authenticating note (v. 17). The prayers echo themes which are central to this letter and which are highly relevant in the pressure and opposition which the believers face.

The missionaries pray to the Lord (Jesus) who is characterised by 'peace' (v. 16) – that is his nature, as a peacemaker, and peacemaking is what he has done for humanity through giving himself to die on the cross. He has brought people into peace with God (Colossians 1:20) and one another (Ephesians 2:15). The letter began with a wish for peace (1:2), echoed here. Peace is vital amid the external and internal threats the church faces. They are being opposed (1:4–6). They are worried by mistaken teaching about Jesus' return (2:1–2). They face the disrupters within their community who cause tensions and sponge off others (3:6–15). It would be easy for them to take their eyes off the Lord himself in all this and to lose the knowledge-in-experience that they have peace with God through Jesus. The missionaries do not pray for them to be given peace by being removed from the problems, but for peace *amid* the problems. And they pray for this peace to be present 'at all times in all ways' – that's pretty comprehensive!

The opening of the letter began with 'grace' and followed with 'peace' (1:2). The team reverse the order here, following their prayer for peace with a request for the Lord Jesus Christ's grace to be with them all (v. 18). A standard Greek letter ending was, 'Be strong!', whereas the missionaries want the believers to experience the Lord's strength, given by his generous love, his grace. That's what will sustain them in difficulties, encourage them in worries and enable them to live in unity. Notice that they pray for 'all of you' – that includes the troublemakers whom they have roundly criticised (3:6–15).

The sign-off is from Paul himself (v. 17), only the fifth time in the two letters where he's contributed individually (see 2:5; 1 Thessalonians 2:18; 3:5; 5:27). As in other letters, this personal note authenticates the letter as genuinely from Paul, for the rest of the letter would be dictated to a scribe (e.g. Galatians 6:11). That would be vital, since the believers were being misled by a letter purporting to be from the missionaries (2:2).

Guidelines

In the political and business worlds, some leaders throw their weight around, humiliate others and make life difficult for those under them. Alas, this is sometimes true in churches, too, as the news has made all too clear in recent years. The Thessalonian disrupters may well have acted in that way, and the missionaries' response to the situation invites us to consider how we lead and are led.

Paul's team did not give the Thessalonians the picture that they were better than them. They worked while in the city so that they weren't living off others (3:7–8), and by this they modelled the Christian lifestyle they advocated (3:9). They weren't unwilling to work (3:10). The trio of missionaries asked the believers to pray for them, both for their evangelistic ministry and for them to be delivered from opponents (3:1–2). They did not pretend all was well and hide the pressures they faced, but instead invited prayer.

It's a great temptation for Christian leaders to live and speak in ways which leave other believers thinking the leaders have no problems and are moving smoothly through the choppy waters of the Christian life. In fact, the reality is more like a swan: although things appear smooth on the surface, there is frantic paddling going under the water! Christians are called to share their needs and challenges appropriately with their fellow believers, and not to give the wrong impression that they're managing fine when they are not. The church is a community of sinners living in a fallen world, and addressing the realities that brings is vital to encouraging and helping others to grow in faith. How do you do that? How could you do it more with appropriate people? If you're a pastor or preacher, how could you speak in ways which open up your weakness and challenges to enable others to share theirs and gain strength?

FURTHER READING

Nijay K. Gupta, *1–2 Thessalonians (New Covenant Commentary Series)* (Cascade, 2016) – If you'd like to dig deeper into this letter, this short commentary provides helpful reflections on the letter's implications for today. You may have looked at it when we studied 1 Thessalonians.

Amos: the lion roars

Peter Hatton

'Faithful,' says the book of Proverbs 'are the wounds of one who loves' (Proverbs 27:6). This, according to some modern interpretations, is not a justification for domestic abuse but a recognition that sometimes, if we truly love, we must be ready to flag up painful truths. It's good to encourage and build up, but often this isn't enough if those we love are to flourish and become the people God is calling them to be; we must also challenge. We are going to read together some of the most challenging words ever spoken on God's behalf to his people, namely those found in the book of the prophet Amos.

Many of these words specifically concern the wealthy, powerful kingdom of Israel – the ten northern tribes who had split around the middle of the tenth century BC from the original 'united kingdom' founded by David and consolidated by Solomon. Two hundred years later, people In Israel thought Amos' message to be nonsense, disproved by the prosperity and success of their state. What right had Amos to say these things anyway? He was not a 'professional' prophet, part of a guild or school, following the family 'trade' of prophecy, but a farmer. Moreover, he was, in their eyes, a foreigner, from Tekoah in Judah, the rump state ruled from Jerusalem by the house of David, a dynasty viewed in the north with deep suspicion. 'Let him denounce the wrongdoings of his own people and stop bothering us!' some cried.

Yet, for Amos, these objections carried no weight. Amos does not regard Israel as a foreign nation but his own, part 'of the whole clan that God brought up out of Egypt' (Amos 3:1). His authority for speaking such challenging words to those he holds to be his own people comes not from any birthright or expertise but from God himself.

We who hear his words today would also do well not to ignore them because they come to us from that past which is, for us, a 'foreign country'.

Translations from scripture are my own. Occasionally, I will refer to the God named in Israel's scripture as 'YHWH'; this name's true vowels have not been revealed and many of our Jewish brothers and sisters find guesses at what they might be offensive.

1 Withering, life-giving words

Amos 1:1–2

Behind these 'words' that Amos will 'see' in the book that bears his name is a vision, that is, a way of seeing; one that perceives things invisible to many others.

On the one hand, Amos sees clearly the realities of his world. His poem begins by acknowledging what has been happening in that world; the sad split in God's people is flagged up by the mention of the two kings who now rule over a land that should be united. Uzziah rules from Jerusalem, in Amos' eyes (and those of the rest of scripture) the legitimate capital; Jeroboam holds sway in Samaria, the capital of the northern kingdom of Israel. He is the second king there to bear this name; the first was the officer who founded the state in rebellion against the (very real) injustices of Solomon's son Rehoboam. Jeroboam II may well have adopted this name on coming to power as a strong affirmation of the legitimacy of the north's breakaway.

The reality of this world (and ours) also includes its vulnerability to what we would call natural disasters: the recent earthquake – possibly one that took place around 760BC – and a devastating drought that could wither even the green pastures of Mount Carmel. We may see in such things merely the happenstance of the material world – although, as we become increasingly aware of the impact of human activity on the created order, we may not now be so confident about the randomness of all 'natural' events. Amos, in any case, would beg to differ. In his eyes, all that happens springs, in the end, from the judgements of Israel's God, *YHWH*. Because he sees this God as deeply enmeshed in the web of all things, Amos views the human world, with its messy politics, as inextricably linked with the 'natural world'. Our actions have far-reaching consequences.

A bleak view? Perhaps, but Amos also sees something more hopeful. God's voice, he asserts, sounds forth from Zion, that is, from Jerusalem (not Samaria), but it reaches deep into the north, to Carmel. So Amos reclaims the holy name 'Israel' for all God's people rather than just part of them. Behind the devastating judgements of his time, Amos sees God at work to reunite and heal.

2 Foreign devils?

We've been told that Amos' words are going to concern Israel, so it comes as something of a surprise when the book's first prophetic judgements are directed at six foreign nations. Modern readers may find it difficult to make much sense out of this list of strange names. The essential thing to understand is that these are territories that surrounded ancient Israel (and Judah). Most were long-standing enemies of God's people. Some, like Tyre and Gaza, were city states; others, like the Aramaean kingdom of Damascus, were larger and more powerful. All represented potential threats even though they could also be, in the complex world of the ancient Near East, on occasions, allies of God's people. For instance, Tyre, under its ruler Hiram, enjoyed friendly relations with Israel in the time of Solomon (1 Kings 7:13–45)

However, the tone here seems unremittingly hostile to these foreigners. Not only does God condemn them for genocidal war crimes, but he also promises to bring appropriate judgements down upon them. Interestingly, only some of the victims here are Israelites – i.e. the unfortunate inhabitants of the border region of Gilead mentioned in 1:3 and again in v. 13. On other occasions atrocities against non-Israelites – forced deportations (v. 6. and v. 9) and the desecration of the bodies of fallen enemies (v. 1) – are regarded as equally blameworthy. We should also note the formulaic nature of these 'judgements'; they are, in fact, 'execrations', ritual curses using a conventional numerical form also found in the book of Proverbs (30:7–33) and outside scripture in other ancient Near Eastern texts.

We may well imagine Amos' first hearers responding with glee to such powerful curses. Ascribing wickedness to others is convenient. Ritual condemnation is even better, confirming that 'God is with us' and we are in the right. Even broad-minded folk like ourselves like to do this, as I have noted in church synods when the readers of a certain popular paper (clue, not *The Guardian*!) have been ritually condemned.

The book knows exactly what it is doing with this 'finger-wagging'. It is setting a trap for those who, perhaps like you and me, love to ascribe all wickedness to those outside our own right-thinking group.

3 All have sinned

Amos 2:4–16

And now the trap is sprung! Unexpectedly the wagging finger turns to point to the very people who had nodded sagely at the condemnation of the wretched foreigners. The sins of God's own people will bring upon them the same fate, defeat and destruction, that threatens other peoples.

However, we might think there is a discrepancy here. The sins alleged against, for example, the Ammonites (1:13) involve atrocities of the worst kind; the other foreign nations stand accused of equally outrageous cruelties. Judah's offence, its rejection of the commands of their God, seems relatively harmless. Israel's misconduct (and the contrast with Judah implies that Israel ought to mean the northern kingdom here, but a certain ambiguity persists – could it mean the whole people of God?) is more graphically described. It involves rampant injustice against the poor (vv. 6–7a) and, it seems, sexual sins of a particularly perverse sort (v. 7b). Interestingly, some scholars suggest that the transgressive practice referred to in this last verse would have been part of an idolatrous ritual. If so, this fits with the accusation in v. 8 that unjust gains are being celebrated in religious centres.

Well, we might grant that this is indeed unrighteousness, but we might think it's pretty small beer compared to genocide and warmongering! Perhaps so, but what is implied here is that God's people are held to higher standards. As the passage points out, they have been marvellously protected and given a land to live in (vv. 9–10). Yet their response has been to suppress the voices and corrupt the exemplary lives that might have kept them on the 'straight and narrow' (vv. 11–12). The consequences will be severe; indeed they will be the same as what foreigners will endure for their more outrageous wickedness.

For both Israel and ourselves, great privileges carry with them weighty responsibilities.

To whom so much was given, of them will much be required.
LUKE 12:48

4 A sober warning

Amos 3:1–12

At the start of this chapter it seems that the ambiguity we have seen so far concerning the name 'Israel' (does it refer just to the northern kingdom or to the whole people of God?) has been resolved. It seems clear that, in Amos 3:1 at least, we are to understand Israel as referring to the 'whole clan [God] brought up out of the land of Egypt'. Moreover, the word 'clan' reminds us that 'Israel' at first referred to one individual, the head of a small, nomadic family, bound into an intimate, personal covenant relationship with God. Those who claim to inherit that person's, that clan's, spiritual legacy may fancy that nothing can break the bond between them and God. They, we, are now confronted with a more sober reality.

For, as we have seen already, such intimacy makes sin more, not less, liable to divine judgement (v. 2). This point is rammed home by the string of analogies that follows (vv. 4–8). These all involve inevitable consequences of actions and all contain an element of threat and menace. Even verses 7–8, which look at first sight a positive affirmation of the prophetic vocation, must be read in this context as a challenge to complacency. The prophets cannot help speaking (even when threatened). This means that we have no excuse; we cannot say God has been silent. He has spoken through the prophets and warned us.

So having made the chilling point that being part of God's family does not give us a free pass to act unrighteously, the book returns to how his judgements work out in practice in a concrete political situation in an actual country, the northern kingdom. Not good news. Even foreigners can see the oppressive violence perpetrated in Samaria, the capital city of the northern kingdom (vv. 9–10). Estranged from God, the city will fall to one of its many enemies (v. 11). There is some hope that something may be retrieved from this calamity, but it is a derisory one (v. 12).

Do you take for granted the riches of his kindness and forbearance and patience?
ROMANS 2:4

5 A slippery slope

Amos 3:13—4:13

The focus remains for some time on the sins of the north, 'the house of Jacob'. We are given an increasingly clear picture of what these involve.

What does Amos see as the root of Israel's sin? We should recall that the first king of the breakaway northern kingdom, Jeroboam I, set up two sanctuaries to rival Jerusalem as places of pilgrimage and worship. One was in the south at Bethel; the other in the north at Dan, also known as Gilgal. His aim was to ensure that his people were not tempted to worship in Jerusalem, for this would strengthen the legitimacy of the house of David (see 1 Kings 13:25–33). At both Bethel and Dan, Jeroboam set up golden calves for the people to worship. Now, in the ancient Near East, idols of storm gods often rode on the back of images of cattle. No such idols bestrode Jeroboam's calves; so he probably argued that they no more breached the commandments against idolatry than did the images of cherubim upholding the 'mercy seat' in Jerusalem's temple (Exodus 25:17–22; 1 Chronicles 28:11).

Amos is having none of this. The altars at the sanctuary at Bethel are, he declares, sinful, indeed worthy of punishment. Pilgrimages to Bethel and Gilgal (Dan) break God's laws. They represent a false religion, one which celebrates the hedonism of the luxury-loving members of the elite in Israel and which leads inevitably to oppression. It will all end in disaster as Israel's armies are crushed, and Samaria itself, abandoned by God, will fall. Again, Israel cannot say they have not been warned. However, the repeated signs of God's anger at the country's blend of nationalism, pleasure-seeking and religion have been ignored. A time will come when that will no longer be possible; Israel will meet God in his awful role of judge.

Some compromises with the things the culture around us honours and worships; a 'pick 'n' mix' approach to religious practices; a belief that God and Mammon can both be served – these can all be plausibly justified with comforting words. The slide into idolatry can begin slowly and with what seem like the best intentions. It soon gathers pace.

6 Where is God to be found?

Amos 5:1–13

How do the true prophets react when they see a nation lost and on the way to ruin? Well, in Amos we see that concern calling forth a fierce anger; but he also feels a deep sadness. Taking our cue from verse 1 we may read the whole book as a lament; it sees the coming fall of Israel through tears, and if its words are strong, it is because that fall is so sad.

Yes, there is also scorn. Israel is on a quest; its people, particularly the well off, scurry from shrine to shrine, from Bethel to Gilgal – even crossing the border to the famous sanctuary at Beersheba in the south of Judah – in search of some experience of God which might bless them. Yet this 'spiritual tourism' (ennobled perhaps by calling it 'pilgrimage') offers nothing real without a genuine search for the living God. Amos mocks this restless displacement activity; these pleasure trips will turn into far longer, harsher journeys into the bitter lands of exile (v. 5).

Where then is the living God to be sought if not at the sanctuaries? He is, strangely enough, to be found close at hand, in the gates of Israel's towns. 'In the gate' (v. 10) – in what was often the only open public space in those densely packed communities – the elders gathered to settle disputes and enact justice. This, Amos proclaims, is the place where God must be truly sought. When justice, especially that justice that aims to protect the poor and weak from the rich and strong is vigorously pursued, then God is found! However, when an elite corrupts for their own ends what goes on in these truly holy places, where in truth-telling God makes himself known, then he, and those who cleave to him, lapse into a rueful silence.

Have we any tears in a time when thousands tramp off to Lindisfarne or Compostela seeking enlightenment, but few will stand with those who are 'no-platformed' if they dare to reprove fashionable orthodoxies?

Justice, justice shall you pursue, that you might live.

DEUTERONOMY 16:20

Guidelines

Ten years ago, Arlie Hochschild, professor of sociology at the University of California, embarked on a radical piece of research. When not teaching at her prestigious elite institution, a stronghold of American liberalism, she immersed herself in the lives of supporters of the Tea Party, the Republican pressure group, in rural Louisiana. Here, she listened to opinions never aired in her *bien pensant* academic circles; dialogued with those she disagreed with; learned to value and indeed cherish some of the many good things she found in a community which was, in many ways, as strange to her as a foreign country. She offers her reflections on this experience in her book *Strangers in Their Own Land* (2016). It ends with a moving plea for people – particularly powerful elite people like herself – in the United States to get out of the 'echo chambers' they feel comfortable in and listen to other voices, strange and foreign though they may seem to them.

This does not mean that we have to abandon all our own deeply held beliefs; Hochschild sought, respectfully, to share with her 'redneck' friends why she remains deeply committed to public spending and government action to promote social justice. What it does mean is that we ought to be prepared to hear those who speak to us words we may find disturbing; that we should strive to discover what God may be saying to us when we venture into strange territory; that we ought to allow our limited horizons to be expanded.

The words of Amos were offered in the hope that they would break the confirmation bias of people who had got so used to comforting voices supporting their way of life that they were incapable of changing it in ways that might lead away from disaster.

- Do we only listen to those media outlets that confirm our existing opinions?
- Are we prepared to truly listen to those we disagree with, seeking to discover what truth we might discover in what they are saying?
- When did we last change our mind about something really important?

1 Coming back to the heart of worship

Amos 5:14–27

Amos now assaults the most cherished traditions of this people.

These include a belief that a day would come when *YHWH*, 'their' God, would bring in a final victory when their many enemies would be crushed. It would be clear to everyone that they themselves were 'on the right side of history'. Amos shares their belief that God does indeed act through all that happens in the world and, yes, their day will come. However, it will not be a day of shining triumph but one of gloom; their sins will find them out; they will endure a dark fate at the hands of their foes.

Do they imagine that their supposed devotion to *YHWH*, their lavish sacrifices, will guarantee his support when they need it most? They should think again. Indeed, God 'abhors' all they offer (vv. 21–23).

These are radical claims. That the whole sacrificial system is a sort of displacement activity that points people away from where they might truly find God is in some tension with (scholarly speak for 'it completely contradicts'!) much in the rest of scripture. Exodus, Leviticus, Numbers and Deuteronomy, for instance, give good warrants for believing that the answer to the question in verse 25 is – in spite of what Amos implies – 'yes'. In fact, at the centre of Israel's worship in the desert were the sacrifices offered in a tabernacle that was the pattern for later temples.

Sometimes a prophetic word must be 'over the top' if it is to be heard. Because he sees so clearly the huge gap between what happens within the sanctuaries and what happens outside them, Amos seeks to shock Israel out of complacency. He repeats his earlier claim that only when justice is done can God be known (v. 24). Without righteousness, even the most correct liturgy leads to idolatry, as verse 26 implies.

Do we care more about an hour on Sunday than what happens in a 40-hour (or more!) working week?

2 Is it me, Lord?

Much here is, by now, familiar. Once again, we hear fierce denunciations of the luxurious lifestyle of the elite in both Israel and Judah, of their confidence in their own military strength (soon to be revealed as misplaced). There are, however, some shocks.

In verse 5, even the revered King David, the 'sweet singer of Israel', is linked with those who spend their ample leisure time strumming on lyres while gorging on delicacies.

Aren't these criticisms unfair? What, after all, is wrong with a bit of luxury? Don't many of us lead lives which are comfortable, indeed very privileged? If we join in condemning these ancient hedonists, isn't our outrage simply 'virtue signalling'?

Well, perhaps so; although we should note that it is not prosperity itself that Amos regards as blameworthy. No, his accusation is that these particular comfortable lives are funded by oppression, by injustice so flagrant it defies common sense (v. 12).

Certainly, the rest of scripture, in particular the book of Deuteronomy, whose moral stance is so close to that of Amos, often sees prosperity with the 'fear of *YHWH*' as both possible and a sign of God's blessing (e.g. Deuteronomy 7:12–16; 28:1–14; compare Proverbs 13:11). Of course, we may suspect that those 'at ease' in both Samaria and Zion also thought that their comforts were the fruit of hard work, enterprise, a readiness to accept responsibility in the service of others and a sign of divine blessing.

So tyrants deceive themselves. Are we also deceiving ourselves? A real question, and one that may not be easy to answer truthfully. Some other questions might help us, for instance:

- Do we enjoy all our things as gifts from a gracious God, held in trust and to be passed on whenever others have need of them?
- What would we do if our wealth was threatened?
- Are we aware of where our savings and pensions are invested?
- Might it be an act of obedient discipleship to raise some awkward questions at the AGM of a pension fund or a company we hold shares in?

3 Passion… and compassion

These verses include some of the harshest in the entire book. Moreover, this time it's personal.

Amaziah, one of the most senior clerics in Israel, puts Amos' life in danger by informing the king of what he has been saying, and, what's more, he challenges the legitimacy of the prophet's calling (vv. 10–12). Is Amos' response simply vindictive? On the one hand, there is the humility in his claim that he is not a 'professional' but a simple working man, only prophesying by direct divine command (vv. 14–15); on the other, is the bitter fate foretold for Amaziah and his family (vv. 16–17) motivated by rancour and personal venom?

Those of us who have been entrusted with pastoral responsibility in Christian communities may even feel a certain sympathy with Amaziah. A – perhaps eccentric – brother or sister claims they have a direct line to the Lord; how do we know their words truly come from him?

Deuteronomy 18:21 raises the same question, to which 18:22 responds – true prophetic words can be recognised because they will be validated by later events. Accordingly, Amaziah's real sin was his rush to judgement. Had he listened carefully and reflected, he would have heard, behind the condemnations, something that might have led him to give Amos the benefit of the doubt.

For just before this difficult passage are words that imply the prophet is not, at heart, motivated by indignant disgust at Israel's failings, but by pity. Twice in verses 1–6, Amos is so horrified by the appalling disasters threatening the people that he cries out to God on their behalf; and his pleas are heard! Of course, that does not mean that Israel does not continue to be held to account, but in full awareness of the standards of God's justice (vv. 7–8), Amos still dares to intercede for the people. He feels for them in their weakness even as he deplores their sin.

If we are quick to speak (or tweet) condemnatory words about others, to denounce or even to 'cancel', we should recall our own frailties. Righteous indignation without compassion clouds judgement; it does not come from the Lord.

4 The sense of an ending

As if in response to Amaziah's challenge, the denunciations of Israel's sin reach a new crescendo. Again, the charges levelled have two main heads. On the one hand, injustice (vv. 4–6); on the other, false, idolatrous religion (vv. 11–14). We should note that here, as elsewhere in scripture, these two things are intertwined. Those who have no real fear of *YHWH* and are not fed by his word see no reason why they should not prioritise their own desires over the needs of others. Why not, if 'the only hereafter is what we're here, after'?

Mixed in with these accusations are God's words spelling out what must now follow. Much of what God says here, and indeed in the entire book, is summed up by what Amos is shown in verses 1–2. What does he see? The usual translation is 'a basket of summer fruit', but a more literal rendering would be 'a basket of summer (Hebrew: *qāyits*)'. A vision, then, of the prosperity of harvest time? In reality it is a sign of something that sounds similar in Hebrew to 'the end' (*qēts*), which now draws near for Israel. What looks like a sign of flourishing, of health, is in fact, God knows, the last flush of the body of someone whose death approaches.

This pun, which, as said, sums up so much of Amos' message, prepares the way for the dark reversals that will follow – the flip from rejoicing to mourning (vv. 3, 10) and from light to darkness (v. 9). Indeed, the land will be flooded, just as Egypt is inundated by the Nile (v. 8), but these 'waters' will not bring life and fertility (as does the Nile's flood) but destruction and disaster.

What is the reality behind the unparalleled prosperity of much of our own world? How long can it last? Are we ready for it to end?

Whenever they say 'peace and security', then suddenly ruin will come upon them.

1 THESSALONIANS 5:3

5 It's not all about you

Surely things cannot get any worse. Could Amos express God's anger at his sinful people any more strongly? It appears he can. Indeed, the book seems to be coming to a climax in a frenzy of divine wrath.

YHWH is depicted as standing beside the altar, the very place where Israel enacted in sacrifice its claim to have a special relationship with God. However, rather than receiving their offerings with satisfaction, he is pulling down the fabric of the (idolatrous?) shrine upon those who have come to worship. Then he launches himself in pursuit of any survivors, seeking them out to destroy them, no matter where they may try to escape.

Given that this God is understood as enjoying total mastery over the entire cosmos (vv. 5–6), the prospects for Israel appear totally bleak.

Should they cry out, reminding God of his ancient covenant relationship with their ancestors? Amos has him forestall such a plea in words that stand in some tension with his own words in 3:2, and much else in scripture (e.g. Deuteronomy 32:9; 1 Chronicles 17:21; Psalm 105). It seems that Israel's relationship with God is not, in fact, unique. Other nations (v. 7) can tell similar stories of divine deliverance!

With this radical claim, the lowest point for Israel is truly reached. However, even here there is some ground for hope. Amos does not say that the covenant with Israel has been set aside, only that other nations are also part of the divine purpose. Moreover, it now seems that there are limits; the destruction will not be total (v. 8). Yes, there will be a 'sieving'; a time when God will shake and test his people. However, the 'pebbles' (those who have remained faithful?) will not fall through the sieve to be lost in the dirt. No, it will be the 'sinners', those who think they cannot be touched by disaster, who will fall (vv. 9–10).

Do we have a sense of entitlement because of how God has dealt with us, or the group we belong to, in the past? As Amos makes plain, he has no favourites (compare Romans 2:11). Yet those aware of their sin and their weakness, who cling to his Son, may have hope.

6 It will all end well

'Woe and thrice woe' has been, it seems, Amos' unrelenting message. Now, in the closing verses, a new and unexpectedly hopeful note is struck. Why is that?

Well, the standard scholarly explanation is that the book was edited, perhaps centuries after Amos, by a Judean scribe. The scribe wanted, it is proposed, to co-opt Amos into the sort of optimistic message about return from exile (in Babylon) and restoration found, for instance, in the closing chapters of Isaiah. Hence the references to the 'booth of David' (Judah/Jerusalem?) in verse 11.

This may seem a plausible conclusion, but is it the only one? After all, sudden changes, indeed reversals, of feeling are common enough in biblical poetry. Psalm 22 is bleak, yet ends on a note of confidence in God's saving power; even Lamentations contains a few verses at its heart (Lamentations 3:22–36) that express confidence in God's steadfast love.

Nor do the references to David, and even return from exile, lead to the inevitable conclusion that the poem's end was added later. After all, Amos was from Judah himself and, as we have seen, often 'Israel' has included Judah in his book. Indeed, the unique phrase, the 'booth' (*sukkah*) of David (rather than the much grander 'house') is telling here. On the one hand, it subtly undermines the pretensions of the Davidic monarchy (compare the thinly veiled criticism of David in 6:5 – Amos is no Judean 'my country right or wrong' nationalist). On the other, it makes links with the 'feast of booths' (*sukkot*), when Israel's wanderings in the desert as a pilgrim people with *YHWH* as their only king were recalled (Leviticus 23:39–43). Moreover, exile is the fate that threatens the disobedient throughout.

The hope expressed as the book ends is, accordingly, not the shallow optimism of the sinners Amos has critiqued throughout it. Bleak times lie ahead for God's people. Yet because *YHWH* is the God who brought Israel out of Egypt, he will act again to redeem and save them. Fascinatingly, the final redemption will be something wonderful but strange, even paradoxical (v. 13). Those who see all Israel's prophetic words as fulfilled in Jesus of Nazareth, 'God with us', would expect nothing else.

Guidelines

In his sketch 'Is God gay?', atheist comedian Ricky Gervais 'deconstructs' the story of Noah and the flood. God, says Gervais, commits genocide while having a 'hissy fit'. A friend of Gervais had commented that this makes 'God sound gay', but Gervais dismisses this 'because God hates gays'. No doubt some might be shocked by this somewhat outdated (2010, though still popular on the net) riff. However, it would be its attitude to sexuality, rather than its blasphemy, that would be, perhaps, found most offensive.

Indeed, many believers would tacitly agree with Gervais' assumption that God's anger is deplorable. During my long pastoral ministry, the devout told me often that they found the Old Testament very hard because it 'preaches a wrathful God'. Having read through the book of Amos, might we not feel that such a conclusion is difficult to resist? When God threatens dire punishments for minor cultic irregularities, hasn't he 'lost it'?

What however, if we were to understand God's 'wrath' as the passion that burns in his heart for justice to prevail, rather than him losing his temper? Would we not want a human judge to be doing their job not for the power, status and wealth it affords them, but because they yearn passionately to see justice prevail for the weak and powerless? Might we not regard what look like threats as warnings? As revealing what must follow once an idolatrous world view – one in which self-interest, hedonism and the pursuit of power are sanctified – drives out true religion in a land? Indeed, most challengingly, might our disquiet at divine anger in scripture be an index of our own complacency at – indeed, complicity in – such idolatry?

Yes, Amos knows, like the apostle Paul, that 'the wrath of God is revealed from heaven on all humanity's false religion and unrighteousness' (Romans 1:18). However, this divine passion to see right prevail is married to his compassion. It serves his real, ultimate purposes: to save, to heal, to restore, to bless.

FURTHER READING

The Bible Project, 'Amos', **bibleproject.com/explore/video/amos**.

John Goldingay, *Daniel and the Twelve Prophets for Everyone* (SPCK, 2016), pp. 117–44.

James L. Mays, *Amos* (SCM Press, 1969).

God's surprising kingdom: twin parables

David Spriggs

The parables of Jesus have been recognised as both special and significant. Special because they appear to give us so much insight into the mind and heart of Jesus and because they have many qualities which appear very distinctive. Significant because they are 'parables of the kingdom' and provide much of the teaching of Jesus on this central message at the heart of his proclamation.

But they are also intriguing. They have been the subject of endless sermons over the centuries as well as numerous, often groundbreaking, academic studies and, in previous generations, many more devotional books. Yet, given all of this, they still remain controversial as to their 'proper' interpretation (e.g. from allegory to only one point per parable). The way in which they are introduced in all the synoptic gospels indicates that this may well have been the case from the earliest times (see Mark 4:11–13; compare Matthew 13:13–15; Luke 8:9–10). A glance at any substantial commentary reveals the complexities and variety of interpretation which have been attributed to these verses.

In this week's notes we focus on another fascinating and distinctive aspect of Jesus' parables, namely that some of them appear in pairs – apparently to make the same point with different stories. These are sometimes appropriately called 'twin parables'.

In addition to twin parables, there are 'twin sayings', for instance Matthew 7:6 and 12:31–33. These recall the 'parallelism' in the Psalms (e.g. Psalm 25:4; 58:7) or even more so some of the Proverbs (e.g. Proverbs 6:27–28; 7:2–3). Does this suggest that Jesus developed his 'twin parables' from these wisdom sayings? The line between such pithy sayings and short 'twin parables' is not easy to draw.

Unless otherwise stated, Bible quotations are taken from the NRSV.

1 The patch and the wineskin

Mark 2:18–22; Matthew 9:14–17; Luke 5:33–39

We start with a fascinating example of a twin parable. First, it is the only twin that appears in Mark's gospel (although compare 3:23–27). Second, unusually, both Matthew and Luke have both parables and in the same order. Third, we might question whether they are 'parables', as only Luke refers to them in this way and none of them have the usual kind of introduction. Finally, again unusually, the context in all three gospels is the same, namely the question as to why Jesus' disciples don't fast while John the Baptist's and the Pharisees do.

The two parables seem close parallels. They are about the danger of mixing new and old (new cloth sewn on to old cloth and new wine put into old wine-skins), the implication being that Jesus is the 'new' and cannot be easily integrated with the old. There is a possible further implication that if you try to do so, then Jesus is likely to destroy or damage the old and that the new will itself become wasted. Is there here an echo of the previous saying about the bridegroom being taken away from the disciples?

But the parallels are not quite complete. The new piece of cloth is not destroyed – it damages the old, whereas the new wine would be wasted. There are subtle variations in Luke's accounts, which may be seeking to cope with this imbalance. Mark and Matthew describe the cloth as 'unshrunk' and explain that it will 'pull away from the cloak, and a worse tear is made'; here the focus is on the old cloak and not the new cloth. Luke, on the other hand focuses on the new piece. He describes it as being torn 'from a new garment' and 'the piece from the new will not match the old'. If the new piece of cloth is already part of a garment, then once it is cut, the new garment has been wasted. The part torn from it leaves a hole and the old is not restored either. Hence, in Luke's account the parallel to the old wineskin and new wine both being wasted is much clearer. However, it leaves another problem. A new garment is better than an old one, whereas new wine isn't. Interestingly, Luke adds a saying to this effect. But it undermines the implicit claim that Jesus is the 'new'.

2 Mustard seed and yeast

Matthew 13:31–33; Luke 13:18–21; Mark 4:30–32

These two parables both occur in Matthew and Luke, and in the same order, whereas only the 'mustard seed' occurs in Mark.

The context of Matthew and Mark is similar but not identical – the two parables are preceded by the parable of the sower and, in Matthew, the weeds among the wheat or, in Mark, the growing seed. Luke's context, on the other hand, is very different.

Mark's context suggests that the mustard seed is one of several arable parables emphasising the (inevitable or mysterious) growth of God's kingdom that had been collected together. Then the 'yeast' provides a domestic parallel – also stressing the impact of the kingdom permeating the surrounding community. With Luke, it has been noticed that he likes to pair 'male' and 'female' elements in all kinds of ways – here then, the sowing representing a male role and the breadmaking a female one.

It is normally understood that the reference to the 'birds of the air' nesting in the tree which has developed from the mustard seed is, as in rabbinic writings, a reference to the Gentiles finding space within God's kingdom. Equally the 'tree' is a common symbol for a powerful kingdom which protects its vassal states (see David Hill, *NCB Matthew*, p. 233).

The 'yeast' has a less auspicious background. It is normally seen as pernicious, unclean or polluting. At one level this is inappropriate here. So, taken in the context of being a twin parable, where each helps with the interpretation of the other, the overall emphasis is positive and indicates the powerful, if unseen and (at one level) unexpected, consequence of transforming the whole batch of dough into edible bread. However, the Lucan context may indicate that this negative aspect of understanding should not be dismissed too quickly. Luke places it following the healing on the sabbath day in the synagogue. Jesus was rebuked for this by the 'ruler of the synagogue' and possibly others – see verses 15, 'hypocrites' (plural), and 16, 'all his opponents' (plural). Jesus was regarded as 'yeast', a dangerous and corrupting influence. He may have been using it sarcastically against himself, but then pointing out the great and good work that it achieves. As Tom Wright indicates, 'a small helping of leaven… seems insignificant and ineffectual. One healing of one woman – but every time you break the satanic chains… another victory is won which will go on having repercussions' (Tom Wright, *Luke for Everyone*, SPCK, 2001, p. 167).

3 Buried treasure and pearl

Matthew 13:44–46

Here we have two very succinct parables which have no parallels in the other synoptic gospels. However, unusually, both of them appear in the gospel of Thomas. There they are separated from each other and appear in reverse order. As the wording contains variations which provide a somewhat different take on the story, it is worthwhile noting these passages.

Jesus said, 'The kingdom is like a man who had a treasure hidden in his field and did not know it. And when he died he left it to his son, who also knew nothing about it, and accepted the field and sold it. And the buyer went, and while he was plowing, he found the treasure. And he began to lend at interest to whoever he wished.'

Jesus said, 'The kingdom of the Father is like a merchant who possessed merchandise and found a pearl. The merchant was prudent. He sold the merchandise and bought the pearl alone for himself. You, too, are to seek for the treasure that does not fail, where no moth comes near to devour and no worm destroys.'

Translation from B.R. Throckmorton Jr, *Gospel Parallels*, fourth edition (Nelson, 1989), p. 80 note.

The Thomas version gets round a 'moral' problem that is often raised in sermonic material, namely the legitimacy of the man who stumbles on the treasure in someone else's field, then 'deceives' the owner by reburying it, before going off and buying it. In the Thomas version the man buys the field and only then, as he works the land, does he find the treasure – so it seems less of a dubious move. He also re-invests his find and gets interest, echoing other parables of Jesus where this tactic is commended.

The Thomas version of the merchant discovering the pearl is similar to Matthew's, although it is not as clear in Thomas that the merchant is seeking for pearls.

In both parables in Matthew, the emphasis is on the willingness of the person to throw caution to the wind to obtain the desired end. This fits with the recurring theme of Jesus that obtaining the kingdom requires, but is well worth, giving up everything else. This point is, to say the least, 'muffled' in the Thomas version.

4 Safeguarding your real treasure

Matthew 6:19–21; Luke 12:32–34

Should these sayings count as 'parables', as there is only an implied story? Such a story could have been along these lines:

A wealthy man bought much fine cloth and collected gold and precious jewellery, which he kept safely in his great house. He said to himself, 'I have an abundance of riches, I can take my ease.' Then one day he sent his steward to check on his abundant treasure. The steward discovered the cloth was ruined by a moth infestation and thieves had stolen the treasure. When the steward reported this to his master, his master was totally distraught.

What we do have is two (at least) 'accounts' of the vulnerability of human treasure. In Matthew the dangers – both 'moth and rust', which would destroy expensive cloth and garments, and theft – are stated twice, negatively and postively (that is, how to avoid these risks by investing in God's kingdom). In Luke we have the reverse order, namely the danger of thieves and moths (no mention of rust), but only in the positive form.

We saw that the gospel of Thomas has a similar statement: 'Seek for the treasure that does not fail, where no moth comes near to devour and no worm destroys.' This indicates a further danger, as Thomas adds worm to moth and rust! But there is no mention here of robbery. Thomas puts it in the positive form.

But what exactly is the meaning of these lines? What constitutes the 'treasure(s) of heaven'? Luke tells us that, given our security, which we have because God delights to give us his kingdom, we should sell our belongings and give to the poor. Matthew precedes his sayings with the directive to fast in secret, so that our Father, who sees what is done in secret, will reward us. But earlier (Matthew 6:1–4) he had dealt with alms-giving to the poor in a similar way. The content, then, may not be dissimilar. However, Matthew seems to emphasise the trust in God required rather than the beneficiaries – the poor. But Luke's final verse indicates the need for trusting God too.

5 The coin and the sheep

Luke 15:1–10; Matthew 18:10–14

In Luke's gospel these two parables present a very clear example of a twin parable. The structures are very similar. They describe the situation of the lost and the steps taken to search for it and end with it being found. In both cases the 'story' is presented in terms of a question: 'Which one of you…?' 'What woman…?' Even this difference is interesting. The male tale is presented as being addressed to the hearer directly, whereas the female story is less direct. Clearly these offer an excellent case of Luke's interest in male/female pairs. But do they also indicate that in the original context they were addressed primarily to a male audience?

Matthew only recounts the story of the lost sheep, which in many ways is close to the Lucan version but is less direct, 'If a shepherd…', and in this sense is closer to the introduction for the coin in Luke. The major difference *within* the story is that there is no calling of friends together to celebrate the success in Matthew. However, the major difference lies outside the story – in the context and by implication the referent for the sheep and the coin. In Luke the context is the complaint of the Pharisees about Jesus being with sinners, whereas in Matthew it is 'despising these little ones' (see also 18:1–6). Who are these 'little ones'? In Matthew they are probably young (in terms of length of commitment to Christ rather than physical age) and therefore vulnerable disciples. Hence it is not easy to reconcile the purposes in Matthew and Luke which the parable is addressing.

Given these different contexts, the applications of the parable are different too. For Matthew the story indicates God's commitment to the 'little one'. In Luke it is to those who are not yet safely in the fold (e.g. tax collectors). Luke's purpose seems to fit better with the story than Matthew's. Something along the lines of 'make sure you don't allow the new lamb to slip out of the fold and so become lost' might be more apt for Matthew.

Certainly, Luke's stories of the lost-found underline the status and opportunity for those who are not yet within the kingdom; the seeking corresponds to Jesus' 'welcoming and eating with sinners' that so affronted the Pharisees. Both responsibilities are properly the mandate of the people of God.

6 The tower and the battle

Luke 14:25–35

These parables are introduced by Luke as follows:

Now large crowds were travelling with him; and he turned and said to them, 'Whoever comes to me and does not hate father and mother, wife and children, brothers and sisters, yes, and even life itself, cannot be my disciple. Whoever does not carry the cross and follow me cannot be my disciple.'

Such serious demands are recorded in the other gospels too, of course, but neither Matthew nor Mark records either of these parables.

We note again that Luke implies that Jesus is addressing male disciples. In spite of Luke's fondness for male/female pairs, it is only 'wife', not 'husband and wife'! The two stories are addressed to the hearers ('Which of you…'), although, as with the sheep and the coin, the second twin is less direct, 'Or what king…' This may reflect the status of those who were listening. They were more likely to be in a position to build a tower than to start a war.

The twin stories commend careful calculations of the costs and resources available to avoid shame; both are (unusually) male-focused. The building of a watch tower would be the farmer's responsibility, not his wife's, and the gathering of an army plus the decision to rebel would be the king's.

But while neither Matthew nor Mark has parables to challenge glib discipleship, they do have incidents. Matthew 8:19–22 (paralleled in Luke 9:57–60) tells us:

A scribe then approached and said, 'Teacher, I will follow you wherever you go.' And Jesus said to him, 'Foxes have holes, and birds of the air have nests; but the Son of Man has nowhere to lay his head.' Another of his disciples said to him, 'Lord, first let me go and bury my father.' But Jesus said to him, 'Follow me, and let the dead bury their own dead.'

It would have been quite easy for Jesus to construct 'twin parables' about animals having their secure places and another about funeral arrangements. But presumably he didn't.

The interpretation of carrying the cross and following Jesus is clarified by Luke after the parables as 'giving up all your possessions' (v. 33). While this is another of Luke's special emphases, it is also implied in the other gospels (see Mark 1:16–20) and, significantly, by Matthew's 'incidents' above.

Guidelines

- As we have proceeded through this week looking at twin parables, do you sense that we are in close touch with the message of Jesus?
- What important issues/themes have you noted from these parables? Do these present challenges for us in the same way they did for Jesus' hearers? Or do the different contexts make direct applications different for us? What effect might this have when we come to preach on them?
- Consider the range of situations that Jesus draws on for his 'parables'. In what ways do you think these reflect the contexts of his listeners? Is it noteworthy that Jesus used situations that were the domain of women? Are there lessons we can learn for our preaching or teaching, when it comes to illustrations?
- Either select a parable from the synoptic gospels that does not have a twin and then write up a possible twin you can imagine Jesus might have used; or rewrite one of his twin parables for a contemporary audience. Bear in mind that Jesus drew his parables from the common life experiences of his audience, seems to have had a preference for ensuring that there was a balance of male and female situations and often used humour in his characterisation.
- In what ways do you think that having 'twin' parables might help us navigate the interpretation of Jesus' parables more sensitively? Do you think they can provide clues about the limits of over-interpreting (or under-interpreting!) the details in any parable?
- We have noted that sometimes the parables are given different contexts in different gospels and this may even have re-shaped the details of the parable or the implied meaning of it. These changes are usually attributed to the work of the writers of the gospels or the process of oral transmission which preceded this. Do you think it possible that Jesus used the same/similar stories for different purposes on different occasions? Have you ever been aware that preachers you have heard have done this?

FURTHER READING

Kenneth E. Bailey, *Jesus through Middle Eastern Eyes* (SPCK, 2008).

C.H. Dodd, *The Parables of the Kingdom* (Collins, 1961).

Joachim Jeremias, *The Parables of Jesus* (SCM, 1963).

Martyn Payne, *Messy Parables* (BRF, 2017).

Life after death

Henry Wansbrough

Biblical thinking on life after death developed gradually, under the progressive revelation of the Holy Spirit. At first Abraham and his descendants conceived the dead as being absorbed again into the stem of their ancestors. Despite their nomadic wanderings, the dead should be buried in one family burial plot. Abraham bought one for his wife and family at Hebron, which then became the tribal centre. Then the idea of Sheol developed, a grim place of half-life, where the dead had no strength even to praise God.

Gradually, the idea developed that God loves his servants so much that he can never wholly desert them. Only in the last two centuries before Christ did a solution begin to dawn. This came in two ways. One way was through philosophy: the body may decay, but the soul is immortal and is harvested by the Lord. The other way is that the bodies of all human beings will rise again, either to reward or to punishment. Then Jesus brings the message that he is the resurrection and life, that all who believe in him and adhere to him in faith will have eternal life. The New Testament gives us little indication of what this life will be.

Only later does the Christian imagination run wild, with pictures of saints seated on clouds and endlessly twanging harps, and of the damned tortured by fire and by horned demons armed with sharp tails and pitchforks.

Unless otherwise states, Bible quotations are taken from the RNJB.

1 The sufferings of Job

Job 19:6–7, 11–27

The book of Job reflects on the problem of unmerited suffering. This comfortable grandee is tested by Satan first by the deprivation of all his family and possessions and then by scabrous ulcers. Three wise friends from the east come to comfort him, urging him to accept the conventional solution, that he is being punished for some secret or neglected fault, which he vehemently denies. Dramatically, the scene is set outside Israel, and the sacred, intimate Israelite name for God is never used; it is as though the special revelation to Israel and the intimate covenant between God and Israel has never occurred. Job rails furiously against God, longing to be free of this unwarranted torment, complaining that God will not even allow him to draw his own breath in peace, begging God to leave him alone, but at the same time clinging to God as his only hope.

At this point (vv. 23–27) he voices his undying conviction that God will somehow preserve him. Job's protest is enigmatic: it is to stand forever, engraved in lead on rock. What does 'From my flesh I shall look on God' mean? 'After my skin has been stripped from me'? Is he to look on God 'from within my flesh' or 'even without my fleshly body'? Who is this 'Redeemer'? The word is normally used of the next-of-kin, the *go'el* who has sacred family obligations to his brother: if I die before my marriage has produced an heir, my next-of-kin must marry my widow and raise up an heir to carry on my name. In his darkness Job is convinced that God will be his *go'el*. Job has not yet reached the idea of a life after death, but clings mightily to the conviction that death is not the end of everything. There is a reason for Job why the words should stay engraved upon rock even when Job is dead.

The same is visible also in other books of the Bible, especially the Psalms. They were translated into Greek some 200 years before Christ, for the sake of Greek-speaking Jews who no longer understood Hebrew and wanted to pray in Greek. Again and again the translation is tweaked: 'save me from death', originally a plea to deliver the psalmist from an imminent descent into Sheol, is seen as a plea that there should be a final rescue from Sheol.

2 Resurrection to new life

The second book of Maccabees was written in Greek. For this reason it was not accepted by Luther into the canon of scripture, following the position taken by St Jerome (the translator of the Bible into the Latin Vulgate), although the Greek version of the Bible was the universally current text of the Bible till about AD400.

Many of the stories of this book are painted up with high drama. Here we have the story of the martyrdom of seven brothers in the Maccabean persecution. The Syrian king Antiochus Epiphanes ('epiphanes' is a claim to be 'god made manifest') attempted to suppress all local religious cults in his empire, such as Judaism, imposing drastic penalties on those who maintained the cult and obeyed the law of Moses. The faithful rallied under a local leader named Mattathias and his sons, the 'Maccabees' ('hammers'), to oppose the orders of Antiochus, even to the extent of martyrdom. This highly dramatic story relates the martyrdom of seven sons of the same mother, heroically encouraged by their mother. It is the earliest evidence of a clear belief in bodily resurrection to new life. Later in the book (12:39–45) the Jewish leader arranges for sacrifices to be offered in the temple for the battle casualties who were found to have carried superstitious charms. The author points out that this too proves a belief in bodily resurrection – once their sin had been purged.

At about the same time we have in Daniel 12:2 evidence of a general resurrection to reward or punishment: 'Of those who are sleeping in the Land of Dust many will awaken, some to everlasting life, some to shame and everlasting disgrace.' The word 'many' in Hebrew and Greek does not have the connotation that some will and some won't; it signifies only a very large number. In this account (but not in the books of Maccabees), resurrection is for the wicked as well as for the good, though with duly varying outcomes.

3 The immortal soul

The book called Wisdom is the latest book of the Old Testament. It stems from the flourishing Jewish colony of Alexandria in Egypt, one of the greatest cities of the ancient world, and was written sometime in the last few decades before the birth of Jesus. It was notionally attributed to Solomon, renowned as the father of all wisdom, according to the convention of claiming authority for a book by attributing it to a revered figure of the past. In fact the author is unknown. This first part of the book considers the final destiny of the righteous and of the wicked. In the first part of today's reading, the wicked are mocking the hopes of the righteous; then the author turns to re-assert these hopes.

The book was written in Greek and the thinking is Greek, for Alexandria was a great centre of philosophy; there were even important Jewish philosophers there, such as Philo. According to this pattern of thought, the human being consists of two elements, body and soul. The body is merely material and is given its form, properties and abilities by the soul. So while the body dies and decays, the soul is left at peace and free to be looked after and cherished in the hands of God – or (for the wicked) to be dispersed 'like smoke before the wind'. So it is the soul that is the true personality of each child of God, and it is the soul that matters and is immortal.

This is a different view of human nature from the Hebrew conception, according to which a person is an animated body, a body into which God has breathed the breath of life. This makes it harder to understand what exactly is meant by rising from the dead. A risen person must have a real body. This is why it is important that Jesus' tomb should have been empty, that the risen Christ could be touched and eat fish, although he was somehow transformed and could enter an enclosed room. The risen person is no will-o'-the-wisp ghost, no passing shadow, but in some sense a real body.

4 The risen body

1 Corinthians 15:35–53

At the beginning of the chapter (vv. 3–5) Paul quoted an already-firm tradition about the meetings with the risen Christ. This was obviously a piece of tradition learned by heart by new converts. It is not in Paul's own style or vocabulary, and he says that he received it and passed it on – in the same way as rabbis passed on their traditions. Now he comes to explaining what is meant. He proceeds by three stages:

1 There is continuity: a grain of wheat produces only wheat, not thistles. I remain the same person, with whatever is needed for continuity.

2 'Body' is an analogical term: there are different kinds of body. Fish, birds and animals all have different kinds of body; any cook will confirm this! Similarly with 'glory': sun, moon and stars each have a different kind of glory.

3 In four ways the body takes on a characteristic of God:
   - From being corruptible, it becomes incorruptible (with God's incorruption)
   - From being contemptible, it becomes glorious (with God's dazzling glory)
   - From being weak, it becomes strong (with God's untiring strength)
   - From being natural, it becomes spiritual (with the Spirit of God).

In all these ways the body moves into the sphere of God. Of them all, the last is the most difficult to evaluate. It does not mean in any way that the body becomes unreal. I take it to mean that the body here and now is physical, subject to the laws of nature or physics; in the resurrection it will be released from the laws of physics and animated by the Spirit of God – whatever that entails.

Perhaps this does not tell us very much; perhaps it does. Fabric permeated by light looks quite different. Mix in a chemical and a substance becomes different. Perhaps I will retain my oddities and the limitations which make me who I am, but these will become a source not of frustration or shame but of delight and of hilarious companionship. My faults, having been utterly acknowledged and utterly forgiven, will be merrily accepted and no longer harmful, but rather a joy to myself and to those around me.

5 Life in Christ

We really do not know much about life after death, that is, we cannot even get near to imagining what it will be like. When Paul had that mystical experience, about which he stutteringly tells us in 2 Corinthians 12:2–6, all that he can really say is that he 'heard unspoken words which no human being can speak'. His hyper-emotional and hyper-logical experience cannot be described in any human language: our concepts are not formed for this. All we really know is that it will be life in Christ, a life that has already begun in us at baptism. The final book of the Bible, the Revelation to John, gives us plenty of vivid pictures of life in heaven, but it is difficult to evaluate these as lived experiences.

In his letter to the Romans Paul takes another starting point. At baptism, when we were plunged into the water – or at least sprinkled, though in the early church baptism consisted of being wholly immersed, three times – we were plunged into Christ's death and rose again to his risen life. Water is a symbol of death and a symbol of life. It is a symbol of drowning in the mighty waters of the sea. For the Hebrews, it was even more threatening, since it was then thought that the world was surrounded by endless deep water, held back (on the second of the six days of creation) only by God's command. Water is also a symbol of life, in that humans, animals and plants are all revived and given new life by a drink of water. So at baptism we are plunged into Christ's death and emerge, revived, into his new and risen life.

Paul uses or invents a whole raft of new words beginning with *syn-* (as in 'synthesis' or 'synchronise') to express this juncture of new life: in this chapter alone 'synburied', 'syngrowing', 'syncrucified', 'synliving'. Our new life in Christ, which will lead on to eternity, wraps us in Christ. A close visible analogy to this 'syngrowing' occurs in some trees (e.g. eucalyptus): the original tree dies, but a new tree pushes up from the roots inside the old, thus giving the old tree new life.

There is a development within the Pauline letters. In Romans 5:10–11 we *have* already been reconciled, but we *shall be* saved by Christ. Later, in Ephesians 2:6–8 we *have been saved* and raised up and seated with him in heaven.

6 Eternal life in the Son

If anything is clear about life after death in the New Testament, it is that God became incarnate in order to bring eternal life. Life after death and eternal life are not, of course, the same thing, for eternal life begins already on this earth in the union of the believer to Christ. The believer is already joined to Christ, and this loving union then carries on beyond death and is eternal. Once we have been baptised into Christ, this life carries through to eternity. Jesus himself repays this bond, 'Everyone who acknowledges me in the presence of others, I will acknowledge in the presence of my Father in heaven.'

In Mark, Matthew and Luke, a man, described variously as young and rich, comes to Jesus and asks what he should do to possess eternal life. Jesus replies that he should sell all he has, give the proceeds to the poor and then come to follow him. Similarly, in the parable of the sheep and the goats in Matthew 25, it is those who care for the needy that will be placed at the King's right hand. In John, however, the personal relationship to Jesus is even more central. In conversation with Nicodemus, all Jesus demands is belief in God's only-begotten Son. In the synagogue at Capernaum, anyone who believes has eternal life, and the bread of life is firstly Jesus' teaching and finally the eucharistic bread who is Jesus.

In today's reading, at the Pool of Bethesda, Jesus says, 'Whoever listens to my words has eternal life and has already passed over from death to life.' The healing was done on the sabbath, and the opponents of Jesus objected to his working on that day. Jesus replies that even God works on the sabbath. Indeed God has to work on the sabbath, for babies are born on the sabbath and God gives them life. Then also people die on the sabbath and God has to judge them. The Son, equally with the Father, exercises the power to give life and to judge. Just as the Father has life in himself and gives life, so the Son has life in himself and gives life, and this life is his own life. Those who are in their graves will hear the sound of his voice and will come out to receive the resurrection of life or the resurrection of judgement.

Guidelines

In the early centuries after Abraham, the picture of existence after death was not very positive. Job, however, impatient as he was of accepted solutions, clings desperately to the conviction that God's love will never desert him. This conviction grows stronger as biblical literature progresses. It is only with the Jewish martyrs for their faith, in the early second century before Christ, that the conviction breaks out into the certainty that God will somehow give them back their lives in a bodily resurrection. Jesus teaches that this eternal life will be in him, and Paul tries to explain the continuity-in-transformation which this involves. The book of Revelation (21:1—22:5) puts this in the wider context of the transformation of creation into a joyful wedding feast, surpassing human understanding, for 'what no eye has seen, and no ear has heard, nor has it risen into the human heart, what God has prepared for those who love him' (1 Corinthians 2:9).

Unexpected advents of Christ

Matthew Knell

This set of six studies looks at unexpected advents of Jesus. Given how familiar the Bible's stories about Jesus are to us now, there is something of a barrier to this essential aspect of many events in Jesus' life. Hopefully as we experience these with those who were present or who were first reading accounts, we can discover joys and challenges afresh as Jesus comes into people's lives.

The six occasions have been chosen because they naturally have an unexpected dimension. One appearance that could have provided an interesting study is in 1 Peter 3, which talks about Christ going and preaching to the imprisoned spirits. Sadly, there are too few verses to form a passage for one of these studies. It is a passage that I love, because it doesn't fit into any neat theology that might be created; it is unexpected. Christianity is about faith seeking understanding, not faith in a constructed theology. Too often we seek to create paradigms of knowledge and spirituality that can discourage a humble faith posture before God and scripture that allows a complexity, beauty and richness that we cannot comprehend.

It is worth noting here as well that appearances of God in the Old Testament – 'theophanies' – have not been included, because we can never have confidence that Christ is indicated in these; the Bible certainly never talks in such terms. T.F. Torrance has provided some framework on the incarnation that is interesting in this regard, but more popular references to this effect carry a great danger in denying the biblical account of the incarnation and thus the nature of God and his revealed salvation.

My hope and prayer is that these studies might help you approach these passages with an element of freshness, that you can see something unexpected about the Lord we worship and serve.

Unless otherwise stated, Bible quotations are taken from the NIV.

1 The obvious one: incarnation

Luke 2:1–20

Our first advent is very familiar, bound to images of nativity plays, Christmas services and carols. It is easy to forget that this narrative is about the majestic theology we find in John 1 of the eternal Word made flesh. So how can we break through our familiarity to experience the wonder that should hit us as we consider the birth of Christ? Let's briefly look at two approaches that might help.

First, a wide-angle lens with the first readers of Luke's gospel. We need a right posture for this. One of us has the writing in front of them to read to us, so we prepare to listen. We're excited to hear a researched account of our Lord and Saviour Jesus Christ. We may have seen or heard another account from Matthew or Mark, but most of our learning has been from stories told in the church by leaders who learned them from others. We don't have nativity plays in our minds; no real answer to the question, 'Who is Jesus?' We do know the power of salvation. We know that only a few decades ago Jesus was walking around, talking to people, eating with them, healing the sick. We're waiting for him to come again and so we treasure every story we come across. We come to Luke 2 with childlike excitement and expectation, amazed at the angels and stunned by the contrasting humble setting for the birth of our Saviour.

More devotionally, we sit with Mary as she ponders all this in her heart. How quickly life can change! Preparing for marriage when an angel turns up to announce that you will be the mother of the Son of the Most High, the prophesied virgin with child by the power of the Holy Spirit. Then the census forces a trek down to a packed Bethlehem, where a manger is the best cot we find for the baby. Not a glorious birth, but then some shepherds appear who had a whole chorus of angels proclaiming the news to them. And here is Jesus, and Mary is his mother who will care for him as he grows up. What that will mean and what he will become is unknown, but this is the task for today, to care for this Saviour who has been born. What does this say both about the God who saves and the people who are part of that salvation story?

2 The Nazareth one: homecoming

Mark 5:35—6:6a

Our advent here is the coming of Jesus to his home town at the beginning of Mark 6, but the preceding verses work well in setting the context and bringing through the impact of Christ's arrival in that passage. There are two degrees of surprise present, one explicit and the other implicit.

The teaching and miracles of Jesus are not expected by those in his home town, who react with this series of questions comparing what they know about Jesus with the man who is before them. The difference between the person they had known growing up and this Jesus leads them to take offence.

The implicit shock is seen when we walk with the disciples through this story. They were called by Jesus after his baptism and return from temptation, and their experience had been wondrous as he taught and healed. Yes, some of the religious leaders had issues with Jesus, but this does not seem to have stopped the momentum of the ministry with crowds gathering. In the first part of this passage we have a high point, as Jesus raises the dead to life with Jairus' daughter.

From there we walk with Jesus to his home town – given the reaction, it seems safe to say this is his first time there since his ministry began. Jesus comes and is rejected by people who have known him for years. We are even told that he 'was not able' to do any miracles there except a few healings because of their lack of faith.

This is a shocking advent of Jesus, to the people in his home town, to the disciples and to us. It is a great warning about expectations and realities. In our faith walks with Jesus, it is all too easy to construct understandings about the divinity and power of Christ that make passages like this difficult to read because his humanity has become merely a shell containing the divine. We dislike and are tempted to change 'was not able' into 'did not' as Matthew writes. Yet scripture demands authority, and this passage is in keeping with the covenantal God revealed throughout the Bible. His home-town folk knew the man but could not make space for the Messiah; we know the Messiah, but do we make space for the man?

3 The lake one: walking on water

Matthew 14:22–36

It has been a busy day that was supposed to be a retreat day. Jesus has heard of John the Baptist's murder and sought out a solitary place, only for the crowds to come to be healed, which took all day. Then there is the great miracle feeding them from five loaves and two fish. After the collection of bits left over, our passage starts with a note that Jesus immediately made the disciples get into the boat and go across the lake while he dismissed the crowd and went up a mountain to pray. The disciples must have been tired, and their experience on the boat doesn't seem to help as it is buffeted by the waves.

This is the context for this next arrival of Jesus, walking across the water to his disciples. In the passage we see three reactions to Jesus' coming, and we are challenged to consider our reactions to this Jesus.

The first reaction is from the disciples, who initially think they're seeing things, declaring Jesus a phantasm ('ghost' is a term that can easily be confused by modern depictions).

Given this confused state, Peter's reaction is fairly impressive, both in his request and his initial action of walking across the water. However, with all that he had so far experienced of Jesus, his faith was not sufficient to protect him from earthly fears, in this case from wind and waves.

The last reaction comes after Jesus is in the boat and the wind dies down, when the disciples worship Jesus as the Son of God. This event has progressed their understanding and faith another step, such that they are able to worship him in this way. However, as we walk on through Matthew's gospel we see that this growing faith is insufficient for them to follow Jesus' teaching or his path as he goes to the cross.

We should be at a different point on our faith journeys, living after the cross and resurrection, after Pentecost, after centuries of church understanding and experience of the faith. Peter had sufficient faith to step out of the boat; the disciples believed and worshipped, giving up their lives in following him as far as they were able. As we see Jesus walking on the water to his disciples, what is our faith response in our minds and in the lives that we live?

4 The violent one: the temple

Here we have a double advent of Jesus, into Jerusalem and then into the temple. For our unexpected advents series, we'll concentrate on the latter, as the triumphal entry is presented more as an organised and prophesied event. However, even there we have a telling question in verse 10 as the city asks, 'Who is this?' For all that Jesus has been doing in Galilee and on his way south to Jerusalem, his fame has not impacted the people of the city with their busy lives. As disciples who follow Jesus, who see the kingdom of God breaking into this world in life-changing ways, we need to recognise that for many around us there are many priorities that push out any need to pay attention to Jesus. For all our confidence in Christ's victory and great celebrations, we may find ourselves faced by people who simply ask us, 'Who is this?'

Jesus' arrival at the temple is far more shocking for those who were there, not something that can be observed and questioned, but turning things upside down, literally and metaphorically. Had there been a plan to turn God's temple into a marketplace, to swap a godly spirituality for an earthly worship? I'm certain the chief priests, teachers of the law and moneychangers would have not only denied this, but also not been aware that such a charge could be brought. The complexities of temple worship and the sacrifices prescribed by the law had led to this situation.

It is easy to criticise the temple system that Jesus encountered, but are there not echoes of this that can come into our churches and private spiritualities? Have all our patterns of worship retained God as the focal point? Does brokenness – whether physical like these blind and lame or mental, emotional struggles – find a place where healing is possible? Do our doctrines and spiritual songs allow children to shout out simple, beautiful truths without people becoming indignant? If Jesus were to come into our places of worship, what would he overturn to call us back to God?

5 The living one: resurrection

John 20:1–20

The biggest issue with this study is choosing which of the three resurrection texts to use, since Matthew, Luke and John all have different elements worthy of our attention. It is a bit sad that we don't have angels in John's account, but we are focusing on Jesus' coming and here we have two unexpected appearances to look at.

The first is to Mary Magdalene. It is good that the church today prioritises the countercultural nature of this first witness to the resurrection, a woman and one who had lived a life of sin. John sets this shock up in the first few verses, with Mary going to the tomb and, finding it empty, going back to the men, who run to the tomb to verify what she has told them. So far things are in order, but then the disciples return home and Jesus chooses to appear to Mary. Churches can stress the teaching that is delivered, normally by trained, faithful leaders, but where are the spaces for everyone to tell their story as a witness to the risen Christ? Mary Magdalene as the first witness should encourage us not only to listen more to women than many churches have done in the past, but also to listen to everyone who has a story to tell. This is the essence of scripture's revelation of the gospel, not in systematic doctrines but in lived situations as people experience God's unexpected presence or struggle with his apparent absence.

The second appearance is to the disciples eating together behind locked doors. Jesus suddenly appears, apparently without going through the door. This is miraculous, certainly, but we need to be careful not to make Christ's resurrection body an optional extra – the deacon Philip was transported by the Spirit in his earthly body in Acts 8. The stress here, and in the later appearance to Thomas, is on the continuity in Christ's body, with his hands and side still bearing the marks of the cross. There is a danger with the risen and ascended Christ that we dissolve his humanity away through this process, yet as the angels declare in Acts 1:11, 'This same Jesus, who has been taken from you into heaven, will come back.' God's miraculous honouring of humanity in the incarnation does not end with Christ's death, resurrection or ascension, but continues, speaking to us of the value of the people God created and the people that he has saved.

6 The future one: second coming

1 Thessalonians 4:13—5:11

Our final advent of Jesus is yet to come – his return to bring us to the eternal kingdom. This is unexpected, despite the continuing fascination of some in the church with trying to calculate a date from timings in the Bible or events in the world. I confess to frustrations with these, because they both disagree with New Testament texts that discourage focusing on times and distract people from the life we are called to live as we await the return of Christ.

We should have confidence in the victory of God and the hope that we now have of life with Christ. In all our talk of ministries in the world and the life we now live by the Spirit, talk of death has become sidelined in the church; yet a grasp of the gospel and the Christian life is difficult without keeping death firmly in view. We should seek to live holy, sacrificial lives now because our identity is in Christ and our reward is to come. Sadly there seems to be little focus on either holiness or self-sacrifice in the teachings and lives of churches in the west today, putting us at a distance from the church of the New Testament or many of the churches through history and around the world today. My life should make sense only in light of a confidence in the return of Christ.

Thus there is a sense in which Christ's second advent should not be unexpected, because it informs the lives that we now live here on earth. Paul does not conclude missionally here – though a fervent desire to reach the lost should arise from a knowledge of Christ's return – but calls for holiness and unity. These are not automatic facets of Christian lives, but results of being alert, looking to the light that is to come. That alertness should drive our spirituality day by day in pursuing Christ and our tasks. This urgency seems somewhat lacking, and too often there is an impression that if Christ returned tomorrow Christians would be rather disappointed given all the long-term plans they have been working on.

How does our identity in the coming kingdom drive every aspect of who we are and what we do each day? What does a real expectation of Christ's return at any time demand from us in the lives we live and in our relationships with each other?

Guidelines

There is a lot of 'comfortable Christianity' these days, services where you know what you're going to get, lives that primarily receive affirmation or encouragement. This series looked at 'unexpected' advents of Jesus, but on reflection that first word seems unnecessary. Reading the gospels, Jesus' appearances and actions were rarely what people expected, and throughout the Bible God never seems to leave people's minds or lives the same.

For any who have been reading their Bibles regularly, perhaps for many years, how can we protect ourselves from being conditioned by our existing understanding to allow scripture authority to change what and how we think and live? Here are a couple of things I found helpful to bring the unexpected through when reading the word.

The first concerns how I pick up the Bible. In one sense, it is a book and can be read and studied as a book; when on a phone it becomes an app, which is worse, particularly when notifications from other apps appear. Things change when I pick up the Bible with others in the church, with generations of Christians who couldn't read or with Christians without access to the Bible because of their society's laws. When I come with a Chinese Christian who needed to walk 50 miles to see a Bible, who struggled to read through tears at holding something so precious, my posture changes and scripture has a life and power I submit to, rather than being something that submits to my studies.

When reading, again it is helpful to read with others, even through others' eyes. Our unity in Christ is a reality rather than a nice phrase, so I can read with a brother or sister in prison for their faith, when the Psalms speak powerfully and lead me quickly to prayer; I can read Paul's letters with those new to the faith whose understanding has not been built into theological structures; or I can read David and Goliath with a child and know the excitement that they experience.

FURTHER READING

Venerable Bede, *Homilies on the Gospels: Advent to Lent* (Cistercian Publications, 1989).

Watchman Nee, *Mystery of Christ* (Van Schaik Publishers, 1997).

Diane B. Stinton, *Jesus of Africa: Voices of contemporary African Christology* (Orbis Books, 2004).

'O Come, O Come, Emmanuel'

Imogen Ball

It turns out that Advent hymns are different from Christmas hymns. The season of Advent has increasingly been taken over by Christmas-come-early. Our hymns often sing of a child born while we are waiting to celebrate his birth. Our diaries fill up with celebrations, carols and parties before the event occurs. Our Advent is squeezed by the expanding Christmas-tide. This is even more the case today. November's Black Friday entices us to think about Christmas presents before we even get to the waiting of Advent. Gone are the days of last-minute Christmas Eve shopping for many.

Yet Advent is distinctive. In the Church of England, the season of Advent begins the liturgical calendar, starting each year not with celebration but with anticipation. Advent invites us to wait for a while. Just as the heavily pregnant Mary waited for the advent (coming) of her son, the whole creation now waits in eager anticipation of the coming of the new, restored creation.

These six studies take some time to stand back from Christmas and reflect on five verses from one of the most popular Advent hymns, 'O Come, O Come, Emmanuel'. These lines echo throughout churches across the country during the precious waiting weeks before we celebrate Christ's birth. Using music to mark and memorialise this season engages our whole bodies in the act of waiting. Each verse of the hymn will be held in turn, using verses from scripture to ground and inspire our reflection on these ancient words. I would encourage you to listen to, play or sing this hymn throughout the week, allowing yourself to sit with the music of God with us, Emmanuel.

Text from 'O Come, O Come, Emmanuel' is from J.M. Neale's 1851 translation and, unless otherwise stated, Bible quotations are taken from the NIV.

1 A bit of history...

Isaiah 7:1–17

The divine title Emmanuel only appears in three chapters of the Bible. Here in Isaiah 7:14 the prophet announces a sign from the Lord. This is the verse taken up in Matthew 1:23. The Hebrew word is repeated in Isaiah 8:8 and 8:10, though the latter is translated as 'God is with us' rather than the title Emmanuel. These chapters of Isaiah are highly contextualised within the unfolding drama of King Ahaz of Judah, the surrounding nations of Syria and Israel, and the Assyrian empire. The complex power plays between these nations and their kings drew Ahaz away from the Lord's provision towards seeking protection from Assyria. Matthew's interpretation of the ancient prophesy sees the child conceived within and born of Mary as Isaiah's sign, Emmanuel.

Emmanuel is literally 'God with us', *Immanu El*. Emmanuel has become a divine title and a divine characteristic alongside other Hebraic titles, such as *El Shadday*, God Almighty (Genesis 17:1), *Jehovah Jireh*, The Lord Will Provide (Genesis 22:14) and *Jehovah Rapha*, The Lord Who Heals (Exodus 15:26). These titles of God give us glimpses of his being. Emmanuel expresses the 'with-ness' of God with his creation. From the garden to the desert to exile to the womb, God is with us across the arc of scripture.

The hymn 'O Come, O Come, Emmanuel' is based on seven sixth-century Latin prayers known as the 'Great Antiphons'. The Antiphons formed the response to the Magnificat during Advent Vespers, one each day between 17 and 23 December. The seven prayers were developed into a hymn, possibly as early as the eighth century, but today we sing John Mason Neale's English translation from the 19th century. Each verse opens with a divine title that parallels with the Latin: Emmanuel (*Emmanuel*), Rod of Jesse (*Radix*), Dayspring (*Oriens*), Key of David (*Clavis*) and Lord of Might (*Adonai*). The following days study five of Neale's verses in turn.

2 'O come, O come, Emmanuel'

O come, O come, Emmanuel, / And ransom captive Israel,
That mourns in lonely exile here, / Until the Son of God appear.
Rejoice! Rejoice! Emmanuel / Shall come to thee, O Israel.

Matthew's birth narrative stands in contrast with the detailed description of Luke's. Beginning with the genealogy, Matthew places the birth of Jesus firmly within Old Testament history. Though the genealogy, and indeed the birth narrative, are distinctly (and unsurprisingly) male, there are several women worthy of mention. Contrasting with Luke 3:23–38, where no women are mentioned, Matthew's genealogy has five: Tamar, Rahab, Ruth, Uriah's wife (Bathsheba) and Mary. The motivation for their inclusion is debated, but similarities are somewhat striking. All five women were likely Gentiles and their marital statuses were unorthodox. Aside from these features, each woman has her own story of God with them, pointing us to God, who is with us, Emmanuel.

Matthew's use of the Isaiah 7 prophesy in verse 23 begins a series of prophetic fulfilments in the first two chapters (2:5–6, 15, 17–18, 23) and a theme of fulfilment across the whole book. The quotation in the Greek differs from the Hebrew in the word translated 'virgin'. The Greek, *parthenos*, is an unmarried virgin, while the Hebrew in Isaiah 7:14, *alma*, is a young woman. The concept of virginity is not carried within the Hebrew word but is used by Matthew in his interpretation. The historical context of Isaiah 7:14 makes immediate Messianic resonances tricky. However, the wider Messianic motifs in Isaiah along with Matthew's use of Isaiah 7:14 suggest that the fulfilment of this prophesy is seen within Mary's virgin conception and birth of Jesus.

Mary's experience of God as Emmanuel was unique. The 'with-ness' of Jesus and Mary in pregnancy begins the 'with-ness' of Jesus incarnate with us. In the womb, the baby is with the mother. The two are tied together, the baby feeding from the mother's body, reliant on her for growth, nourishment and life. God was with Mary as Mary carried Jesus with(in) her. Her body marks the embryonic beginning of God incarnate, God with us, Emmanuel.

The opening verse of 'O Come, O Come, Emmanuel', reflects this prophetic fulfilment of Jesus as the Messiah for the exiled Israelites. The appearance of the Son of God is in his simple, stable birth. The mourning of exile turned to rejoicing as Emmanuel appears and the refrain is sung: 'Rejoice! Rejoice!'

3 'O come, Thou Rod of Jesse'

Isaiah 11

O come, Thou Rod of Jesse, free / Thine own from Satan's tyranny;
From depths of hell Thy people save, / And give them victory o'er the grave.
Rejoice! Rejoice! Emmanuel / Shall come to thee, O Israel.

Tree imagery punctuates our biblical narrative: the trees in the garden of Eden, the burning bush, the trees by rivers (from Psalm 1 to Revelation 22), the mount of Olives and the tree at Calvary. In Isaiah 11, multiple tree imageries emerge: a shoot and stump (11:1a), a branch and fruit (11:1b) and a root (11:10).

The Rod of Jesse is hidden within the translation of Isaiah 11:1. The Hebrew *choter* is unusual, appearing only here and in Proverbs 14:3, and translates as 'shoot' or 'rod' (the NIV obscures this in Proverbs; NRSV and others use the word 'rod'). Considering Isaiah 11's recurring tree imagery, shoot is appropriate. This shoot comes up from the 'stump of Jesse'. This stump is a prophecy of the apparent death of the Davidic kingly line following King Ahaz's unfaithfulness. However, the stump remains fruitful. Long after the tree has been cut down, there remain nutrients within the roots that enable the regrowth of new branches. This messianic prophesy points to Jesus as the shoot, or rod, emerging from Jesse's stump and continuing the Davidic kingship. Matthew's genealogy emphasises Jesus as this rod, with roots embedded within a long line of Davidic ancestors. In Isaiah 11:10 this rod is also the root. The Root of Jesse draws people to himself, standing as a banner for the gathering of God's people. Jesus as fulfilment of rod and root provides the nutrients for growth and is the growth itself from the seemingly dead stump. Romans 11:17–21 takes up this theme. As we are the grafted in and share the root that is holy, we too become holy.

The second verse of our hymn does not expand on the Rod of Jesse but does create the messianic linkage proclaiming the salvation we receive in Christ. Victory over the grave is achieved through another tree, the cross of Christ. It is upon this tree that freedom from Satan's tyranny and salvation from hell's depths are accomplished. This victory moves us once again to rejoicing.

4 'O come, Thou Dayspring'

Luke 1:67–80

O come, Thou Dayspring, from on high, / And cheer us by Thy drawing nigh;
Disperse the gloomy clouds of night, / And death's dark shadows put to flight.
Rejoice! Rejoice! Emmanuel / Shall come to thee, O Israel.

This passage, from the long first chapter of Luke, forms the Church of England's Benedictus, spoken daily during morning prayer. These repeated words broke the silence of Zechariah's muted nine months, matching Elizabeth's pregnancy. The title comes from the opening phrase in the Latin translation, *Benedictus Dominus Deus Israel*: 'Praise be to the Lord, the God of Israel.' These words of praise give thanks for what God has done and prophesy the saving work of God in Jesus Christ. Although Zechariah's song follows the birth of his own son, John, much of the Benedictus is in praise of the long-awaited Messiah.

The reference to dayspring is not immediately obvious in our contemporary versions. Dayspring appears in the KJV in verse 78 but is translated as 'rising sun' (NIV), or in the spoken Benedictus, 'dawn'. The Latin term, *oriens*, is the title of the Antiphon which is placed on the darkest day of the year, 21 December. The Greek, *Anatole*, is also related to the east, and encompasses the rising sun and in some cases a shoot or source. *Anatole* as a shoot connects to the previous verse of our hymn, with tree imagery of the rod and root of Jesse. Dayspring further unites water and light to emphasise the life and death imagery continued in verse 79.

This light and death imagery is obvious within the hymn. The 'gloomy clouds' and 'death's dark shadows' are overcome by the dayspring, chasing and dispersing the darkness in place of its own light. The use of light and dark to represent life and death is extensive. Zechariah's words, proclaiming the Messiah as this dayspring, identify Jesus as the light which responds to the world's darkness. The wider imagery of light and dark, life and death, move towards Jesus as both light and life, the answer to our human darkness and death. As God comes to live with us, Emmanuel, the light dawns in our lives, extinguishing darkness, defeating death and offering eternal life.

5 'O come, Thou Key of David'

O come, Thou Key of David, come / And open wide our heav'nly home;
Make safe the way that leads on high, / And close the path to misery.
Rejoice! Rejoice! Emmanuel / Shall come to thee, O Israel.

Revelation 3:7 echoes the words of Isaiah 22:22, where the 'Key of David' is first introduced. Although the imagery of divine opening and closing is repeated throughout the Bible – e.g. God opening and closing the womb – the specific imagery of a key is unusual. The 'Key of David' signifies the one who opens the door to eternal life. This messianic image is prophesied in Isaiah and taken up in Revelation to the church in Philadelphia. However, the divine title 'Key of David' is not in the text. In Isaiah 22:22 the 'key to the house of David' is placed on Eliakim's shoulder, and in Revelation 3:7 the one 'who is holy and true' is the one who 'holds the key of David'.

The concept of keys in ancient mythology was closely linked with death and the afterlife. The Greek cultic goddess Hecate was known as the holder of keys, who was said to give access to the afterlife and acted as a boundary marker between worlds. Revelation's affirmation that Jesus holds both the keys to Hades (1:18) and the key of David (3:7), stands in opposition to the mythological claims of Hecate. Jesus as the true key holder is confirmed in his own words in John 14:6: 'I am the way and the truth and the life. No one comes to the Father except through me.'

Christ as the 'Key of David', rather than merely key holder, is understood in the Antiphon 'O Clavis'. In the verse of the hymn there is no separation between key and holder, as is present in both Isaiah and Revelation. In line with the other divine titles of the Antiphons and hymn, Christ as the key develops the imagery to suggest that it is Christ's own body which holds the key to eternal life. It is the giving of his very self that enables our access to God. In a second mixing of metaphors (similar to rod and root), Revelation 3:20 goes on to describe Christ standing outside the door, waiting for us to open it. Jesus is both the key to eternal life and the one who waits for our response.

6 'O come, Adonai, Lord of might'

Exodus 24

O come, Adonai, Lord of might, / Who to Thy tribes, on Sinai's height,
In ancient times didst give the law / In cloud and majesty and awe.
Rejoice! Rejoice! Emmanuel / Shall come to thee, O Israel.

Although this verse of the hymn and its related Antiphon are titled 'Adonai', the Hebrew word *adonai* does not appear in the Exodus 24 narrative. Instead, in this passage the English translation 'Lord' relates solely to the Tetragrammaton, the four-letter name of God. Both *adonai* and the Hebrew written letters Y-H-W-H, are pronounced 'Adonai' by the Jewish community and translated 'Lord' in the NIV. Adonai in this case is the name of God, which remains unspoken.

Moses' expedition up the mountain was hugely significant for the Israelite nation and begins a pattern of mountaintop experiences throughout the Bible. In Exodus 24:15–16 Moses ascends and the glory of God descends, settling on the mountain. The Hebrew word for 'glory', *kavod*, is distinct from yet related to *kaved*, the inner organ of the liver and emotional heaviness. This does not change the meaning of God's glory, but perhaps influences the perceived quality of glory, particularly when the glory of God appears to be visibly located, resting upon the mountain. The glory dwelt or settled on the mountain and this verb, *shakhan*, is the root verb for the tabernacle, later set up by the Israelites to be the dwelling place of God.

The relationship between Adonai on the mountain and Emmanuel is profound. Jesus too had several mountaintop experiences: the devil tested him on a mountain; he prayed and taught on mountains; he was transfigured and arrested on a mountain. In addition, the dwelling of God's glory on the mountain is a prophetic sign of the dwelling of God with us. John describes the Word becoming flesh and 'dwelling among us' in John 1:14. The Greek *skenoo*, to dwell, is not dissimilar to the Hebrew *shakhan* of Exodus 24:16. God's glory dwelling on the mountain points towards Jesus and the dwelling of God with us, Emmanuel. Although the hymn does not make this link explicit, the inclusion of Adonai and the final repetition of the refrain 'Rejoice, Rejoice! Emmanuel' brings these two historically distant events into theological unison.

Guidelines

Using the verses of 'O Come, O Come, Emmanuel' together with their founda-tional passages from the Bible is an unusual way to explore Advent. Through the more detailed study of these verses and the questions below, insights and reflections may be drawn that will be carried forward and reiterated each time this inevitable, and beautiful, hymn is sung. These questions stem from the studies themselves but can be explored separately, in groups or alone for further reflection on this topic and more practical application.

- We use the term 'Emmanuel' frequently, especially during this time of year. It may be easy to overlook the significance of 'God with us' as it has become so much part of our language about God. How do you understand God as Emmanuel? What does it mean for God to be with you?

- The repeated and varied tree imagery throughout scripture provides a universally helpful image for readers. Are there other occurrences of tree imagery within the Bible which particularly speak to you? How do you understand Jesus as both rod and root?

- Are the imageries of light/dark and life/death helpful for us to think about salvation? Are there other images which are more relevant or useful today? Why might light/dark and life/death imageries be so closely linked?

- The use of key imagery in the book of Revelation is a response to its contemporary mythologies, such as Hecate the holder of keys. Which divine images from this hymn might help us to respond to our contemporary mythologies and cultural assumptions about life and death?

- How might you approach Advent differently in light of God as Emmanuel, root, dayspring, key and Lord?

FURTHER READING

Mark Boyer, *Caroling through Advent and Christmas: Daily reflections with familiar hymns* (Liguori, 2014).

John Cox, *O Come O Come Emmanuel: To celebrate Jesus' coming with hope for all* (Kevin Mayhew, 2016).

Scott Erickson, *Honest Advent: Awakening to the wonder of God-with-us then, here and now* (Zondervan Books, 2020).

Paula Gooder, *The Meaning is in the Waiting: The spirit of Advent* (Canterbury Press, 2008).

Malcolm Guite, *Waiting on the Word: A poem a day for Advent, Christmas and Epiphany* (Canterbury Press, 2015).

Childhood: nurturing, protecting and forming potential

Kate Bruce

In our formative years the neural pathways are established, which will guide how we relate to significant others, shape our self-esteem, and form the way we feel about our bodies and sexuality. Childhood is a sacred time. Scripture urges caregivers to teach children their faith stories so they know their identity (Deuteronomy 11:19–20). The book of Proverbs, a source book of spiritual wisdom, is addressed to a son by his father. Paul holds up Lois and Eunice as examples of a grandmother and mother who have passed on their faith to their child, Timothy (2 Timothy 1:5). Children need good nurturing figures to help, hear and support, guide and nurture them. Where this is lacking, growth into holistic maturity is – while certainly not impossible – inevitably impeded.

In these notes we will look at a variety of biblical texts which raise themes related to the childhood years, beginning with a reflection on God's creative love for us from our earliest days. We will consider how childhood lays down the roadmap for our attachment patterns, before reflecting on the spiritual openness of the child. There is nothing sentimental here: children are inherently messy, often disruptive and frequently loud, yet theirs is the kingdom of God. We will reflect on the dependent nature of childhood, stressing the importance of adults honouring this vulnerability as a sacred duty. We end with exploration of the calling and competency of children, with all their potential for wisdom, spiritual insight and leadership. As adults, we would be wise to be open to learning from the young, whether our own offspring, those we care for or the inner child we carry within our adult selves.

Unless otherwise stated, Bible quotations are taken from the NIV.

1 Created by God: known and nurtured always

Psalm 139:13–16; Psalm 71

Have you ever gazed at a scan photo of a baby in the womb? There is something incredible as you begin to interpret the image, tracing the shape of the baby, discerning its head, its developing limbs and the curve of the spine. The psalmist addresses God with the thought of his own creation in utero. He pictures God knitting him together within his mother's womb, then changes the verb to describe the formation of his physical body as 'woven together in the depths of the earth'. The psalmist's very existence, like yours and mine, is an expression of the artistry of God. The writer imagines God seeing his unformed body. He is beheld by the other; gazed upon by God his creator.

Much low self-esteem could be healed with more emphasis on the significance of the unborn and the newborn to God. The tiny child that was you or I was beheld by God before birth: seen, known and nurtured in the secret places. Many children are not received in the world with the love that God desires, but this does not alter God's love for them, nor does it diminish God's interest and desire for their good throughout the course of their lives.

Psalm 139:16 could tie us into all kinds of unhelpful knots over predestination. I don't think it means that God plans out the details of our lives with pedantic precision, rendering us mere slavish automatons. Rather, I read this image as a recognition that God, standing outside of time, knows the challenges and opportunities each individual will face. God is not indifferent to our joys and tragedies. He meets us in them. God's care for each child extends through all the days of our lives.

Psalm 71 spells this out clearly. Against a deeply troubling backdrop, the psalmist remembers the God who brought him forth from the womb, looking back to this early dependence to help him articulate hope in God in his old age. To paraphrase the logic of the psalmist, he is saying: 'God, you saw me then. I mattered then. Nothing has changed except that I'm grey-haired now and I'm facing many troubles. You are still faithful, so I will still trust.' Whatever you face today, whatever age you are, you matter because you are a child of God, known and nurtured always.

2 Early childhood: establishing the roadmaps of trust

Psalm 131; Isaiah 49:13–17

Picture a young child. Sleepy, fed and content, this little one sits with a parent, heart to heart, calm and bonded. See the securely attached child. From this safe beginning, reinforced through consistency, the child is developing the inner working models to form secure adult patterns of attachment. The psalmist uses this image to communicate how he sees his soul in relation to God. It's a beautiful picture of one who trusts God deeply and is at peace, held and beheld by God. The writer calls Israel to this secure dependence on God. From this basis, faith can grow and develop, loving relationships form, and hope flourish.

One of the essential roles for caregivers is to give young children a loving, secure base; this sows the seeds for the development of positive relationships with others and with God. But what happens when early relationships are insecure, unreliable or downright abusive? How does the adult from such insecure beginnings ever come to establish a secure bond with others, especially with God? This is the spiritual work of the adult years: to develop trust in God, the faith that God loves without condition and can be relied upon always. This is hard work for the insecurely attached child grown into adulthood. Such wobbly beginnings feed into anxiety, ambivalence and mistrust. It's not unusual to hear people talk about a God of love for everyone else, while behaving as though God was out to get them, as individuals. For those with unhealed attachment patterns, the image of God lurking beneath the surface is of an inconsistent deity who needs constant appeasement.

These verses from Isaiah 49 offer a powerful corrective to the story of anyone who has known abandonment, inconsistency, neglect or abuse. Isaiah reminds us that even if a woman could forget her child or have no compassion for her offspring, God can never forget his beloved. Here is a powerful picture of the God who comforts, who is consistent and will never abandon his children.

Meditating on Psalm 131 and Isaiah 49 offers a healing exercise which can reinforce the positive childhood experiences of the securely attached adult, and offer a corrective to the one who struggles to believe they are worth loving. To the anxious and fearful, God reassures, saying: 'I will not forget you. See, I have inscribed you on the palms of my hands.'

3 Spiritual awareness and the child: out of the mouths of babes

Matthew 21:15–16; Psalm 8

There's a photo my grandmother took of me when I was about three. I'm clutching the hosepipe and watering the roses. She captioned the photo, 'Katie mesmerised'. I was. Mesmerised by the pattern of the water spraying out on the vibrant roses, forming a mini rainbow over soft pink petals against vibrant green leaves. I remember other experiences of being small and feeling attuned to nature. Once sitting on the patio, on my own in the sun, with my eyes closed, I had a sense of being seen by someone or something greater than me. It was a warm and comforting experience. There was something about the sunlight, the sound of the insects buzzing and birdsong, that spoke of a greater meaning and order; at the time it was a felt experience rather than a cognitive interpretation. I wouldn't have known then to name God as the one beholding me, but I look back and that's how I understand the event. Sensory experience and childhood intuition led to a profound spiritual moment.

The psalmist clearly recognises that God creates the world and speaks through it. Can we recapture that childlike sense of wonderment at the created order, that openness to seeking the creator in the creation? Can we nurture children's noticing and curiosity, honouring their spiritual awareness? Perhaps too often this sensitivity is overlooked or dismissed and important spiritual conversations which could teach both adult and child are lost.

Both readings today remind us of the God-given spiritual awareness of the child. I love the scene Matthew paints of children in the temple seeing the wonderful things Jesus is doing and shouting about it. Children shouting? Children praising the Son of David? In the temple? No wonder the measured, ordered, self-important religious leaders were indignant. As Jesus reminds them, 'From the lips of children and infants you, Lord, have called forth your praise.'

4 Let the children come: the kingdom of God belongs to such as these

Mark 10:13–16

It's easy to sentimentalise these verses, picturing quiet, clean, compliant children being blessed by Jesus. Such schmaltz does disservice to the power of the scene, and should be deleted along with the line in a certain carol which claims that 'little Lord Jesus, no crying he makes'. When I baptised my nephew, he was far from placid. He was wriggly and unimpressed, making noisy protestation at my watery blessing. Anyone who has spent time around small children knows that they are often messy and loud, blessed with freedom of expression, mucky hands and a thousand questions. They are alive to all the wonders of creation, from ants to armadillos. The children in my life are curious, humorous and adventurous. In their exploration of places, relationships and rules, they make mistakes, which is how they learn. They lack self-sufficiency. They are not steady on their feet. Tears and laughter are frequent events. The kingdom belongs to such as these.

Irenaeus is reputed to have said that 'the glory of God is a human being fully alive'. Children display this aliveness. Securely grounded, they display radical trust; just picture the child who hurls themselves off the side of a swimming pool into an adult's arms. Emotionally healthy children express the range of their emotions, rather than suppressing and pretending. If adults are to be fully alive and receive the kingdom of God, then we need to learn from our children, which takes humility.

Once, leading a Communion service, I watched as a small child ran freely in the aisle, with such unself-consciousness. She danced up the chancel steps and ducked under the altar rail, coming to see what this strange woman in a white robe was doing. Why does growing up sometimes mean losing spontaneity, anxious not to do the wrong thing and fearing looking foolish? Why does it often mean swallowing emotion and seeming to be in perfect control? In this little snippet from Mark's gospel, Jesus offers us a picture of how to enter the kingdom. Be free. Be curious. Be vulnerable. Trust radically. Religious posturing, pride and resistance will see us on the wrong side of the door into God's kingdom. The height of that door may well be around three-foot six – meaning grownups must stoop to enter. Mitres – metaphorical and actual – are going to fall off.

5 Welcome and protect: honour the vulnerability of the child

Matthew 18:1–6; Ephesians 6:1–4; John 2:13–16

Children need nurture and protection – physically, emotionally, spiritually and sexually. Their vulnerability is sacred. Ephesians 6 balances the call to children to honour and obey their parents with the importance of not exasperating them. Children who are not heard, who are dismissed, teased beyond endurance, caught up in painful 'play fighting' are effectively exasperated; rendered voiceless, powerless and frustrated. Where their spiritual curiosity is dismissed, they experience a form of wounding. Children who are forced into sexual acts are left profoundly harmed, blamed and self-blaming.

A child's body is a sacred space; a sexual act introduced to it or demanded of it is a desecration. Interesting, then, to see Jesus rage in John 2 at the misuse of the temple – also a metaphor for the body. His fury is palpable as he drives out those who commit sacrilege with a whip of cords. How crucial it is for survivors of abuse to know that Christ rages for them and with them, that he welcomes, honours and gives voice to the abused.

In the snippet from Matthew's gospel, we see Jesus aligning himself with children; whoever welcomes the child welcomes him. The gravity of causing harm to a child is expressed clearly in his reference to a millstone and drowning. The language of punishment is strong because the cost of abuse is so devastating. Where the vulnerability of childhood is not honoured, the damage caused is deep and traumatic, and the road to healing demanding.

As a chaplain, I often hear stories of people's lives. Recently, I met a young man trying to deal with flashes of anger erupting in response to relatively small triggers. Whenever the anger flared, his eyes would tear up, causing him confusion and shame. Listening to his story, the root cause of his rage and pain became clear. He'd grown up without the protection of a father figure, with unstable adults around, in a violent context, marred by drug dependency. He had learned to survive on his wits, constantly living in fight-or-flight mode, on edge, burdened with a toxic view of masculinity. His childhood vulnerability had not been honoured; as an adult he bears the scars of this. The hope remains that in honouring the vulnerability of the boy within the man, the door will open to his self-understanding and healing.

6 Calling and competency: never 'just' a child

2 Chronicles 34:1–7; Jeremiah 1:4–10; Luke 2:41–52

Quite a few years back I was involved with a course for young preachers. The youngest we had was 15 years old. It was a delight to see him develop over time and a great pleasure to hear him preach at a major conference when he was in his early 20s. His calling as a preacher was rooted in his childhood, beginning long before he arrived on our course.

Children need people to nurture their gifts, believe in their dreams and encourage them when they feel daunted. Josiah, king of Judah, came to the throne at the age of 8. By the time he was 16, 'while he was still young', he began to seek God. Who helped to shape the young Josiah so that he desired God? Who guided him in these formative years, encouraging him to become a reformer? 'Under his direction' Judah's idols were destroyed, the temple was restored, the book of the law recovered. This young leader grew into one of the greatest of the reforming kings. Called and competent, he was never 'just' a child.

Jeremiah responds out of fear to God's call: 'I do not know how to speak; I am only a child.' God chides him against this dismissal of his calling on the grounds of his youth and assures him that there is no need to be afraid, as he will give him the words and be with him. Do we write off young people as lacking experience for leadership? That would be a mistake. Think of Greta Thunberg – a young, powerful, prophetic woman.

We see childhood potential expressed in Jesus himself, who at the age of 12 is able to converse with learned teachers, showing great theological perception and deep spiritual insight into his relationship with God. We might object that he had the distinct advantage of being the Son of God! However, the point is that what we see in Jesus is a familiar pattern. The seeds of a person's gifting and calling are there in childhood. Do we take this seriously in identifying and developing young people's potential? Where are the youngest leaders in our church and society? How can we encourage and develop them, and are we open to learning from the wisdom of youth?

Josiah, Jeremiah and Jesus – called and competent – none was ever 'just' a child.

Guidelines

- What is your earliest memory of being aware of God in some sense? Call it to mind and walk through the recollection, taking time to notice details.
- Take a slow walk in the countryside and be open to all the sensory experiences around you.
- Write a list of words which in your opinion describe the nature of children. Don't be overly sentimental. Look at the words you have written – and reflect on Jesus saying that the kingdom of God belongs to such as these. Where does this exercise take you?
- Reflect on the vulnerability of children. Recall images or stories you are aware of relating to children who are suffering because of some form of deprivation or abuse. Let these images speak into your prayers.
- Think of the children known to you. Give thanks for their gifts and pray that they would grow into all their potential.
- Think of the children and young people in your community. What are their interests and concerns? How is the church listening to them and engaging with them? How could this process be started or developed?

FURTHER READING

John Bowlby, *The Making and Breaking of Affectional Bonds* (Routledge, 2005).

John Bradshaw, *Homecoming: Reclaiming and championing your inner child* (Piatkus, 1999).

Alice Miller, *The Drama of Being a Child: The search for the true self* (Virago Press, 1987).

Become a Friend of BRF
and give regularly to support our ministry

We help people of all ages to grow in faith

We encourage and support individual Christians and churches as they
serve and resource the changing spiritual needs of communities today.

Through **Anna Chaplaincy**
we're enabling churches to provide
spiritual care to older people

Through **Living Faith**
we're nurturing faith and resourcing
life-long discipleship

Through **Messy Church**
we're helping churches to reach out
to families

Through **Parenting for Faith**
we're supporting parents as they raise
their children in the Christian faith

Our ministry is only possible because of the generous support of
individuals, churches, trusts and gifts in wills.

As we look to the future and make plans, **regular donations make a huge
difference** in ensuring we can both start and finish projects well.

By becoming a Friend of BRF and giving regularly to our ministry you are
partnering with us in the gospel and helping change lives.

How your gift makes a difference

£2 a month
Helps us to develop **Living Faith** resources to use in care homes and communities

£10 a month
Helps us to support churches running the **Parenting for Faith** course and stand alongside parents

£5 a month
Helps us to support **Messy Church** volunteers and resource and grow the wider network

£20 a month
Helps us to resource **Anna Chaplaincy** and improve spiritual care for older people

How to become a Friend of BRF

Set up a Direct Debit donation at **brf.org.uk/donate** or find out how to set up a Standing Order at **brf.org.uk/friends**

Contact the fundraising team

Email: **giving@brf.org.uk**
Tel: +44 (0)1235 462305
Post: Fundraising team, BRF, 15 The Chambers, Vineyard, Abingdon OX14 3FE

Good to know

If you have any questions, or if you want to change your regular donation or stop giving in the future, do get in touch.

Registered with

FUNDRAISING
REGULATOR

SHARING OUR VISION – MAKING A ONE-OFF GIFT

I would like to make a donation to support BRF.
Please use my gift for:

☐ Where it is most needed ☐ Anna Chaplaincy ☐ Living Faith
☐ Messy Church ☐ Parenting for Faith

Title	First name/initials	Surname
Address		
		Postcode
Email		
Telephone		
Signature		Date

Our ministry is only possible because of the generous support of individuals, churches, trusts and gifts in wills.

giftaid it   You can add an extra 25p to every £1 you give.

Please treat as Gift Aid donations all qualifying gifts of money made

☐ today, ☐ in the past four years, ☐ and in the future.

I am a UK taxpayer and understand that if I pay less Income Tax and/or Capital Gains Tax in the current tax year than the amount of Gift Aid claimed on all my donations, it is my responsibility to pay any difference.

☐ My donation does not qualify for Gift Aid.

Please notify BRF if you want to cancel this Gift Aid declaration, change your name or home address, or no longer pay sufficient tax on your income and/or capital gains.

Please complete other side of form

SHARING OUR VISION – MAKING A ONE-OFF GIFT

Please accept my gift of:

☐ £2 ☐ £5 ☐ £10 ☐ £20 Other £ [   ]

by (*delete as appropriate*):

☐ Cheque/Charity Voucher payable to 'BRF'

☐ MasterCard/Visa/Debit card/Charity card

Name on card

Card no. [ ][ ][ ][ ] [ ][ ][ ][ ] [ ][ ][ ][ ] [ ][ ][ ][ ]

Expires end [M][M] [Y][Y]   Security code* [ ][ ][ ]

*Last 3 digits on the reverse of the card
ESSENTIAL IN ORDER TO PROCESS
YOUR PAYMENT

Signature   Date

☐ I would like to leave a gift to BRF in my will.
Please send me further information.

For help or advice regarding making a gift, please contact
our fundraising team +44 (0)1865 462305

Your privacy

We will use your personal data to process this transaction.
From time to time we may send you information about
the work of BRF that we think may be of interest to you.
Our privacy policy is available at **brf.org.uk/privacy**.
Please contact us if you wish to discuss your mailing
preferences.

Registered with

FUNDRAISING
REGULATOR

 Please complete other side of form

Please return this form to 'Freepost BRF'
No other address information or stamp is needed

GL0322

Overleaf… Guidelines forthcoming issue | Author profile | Recommended reading | Order and subscription forms

Guidelines forthcoming issue

Guidelines looks set to have some fantastic contributions as we go into 2023!

We have the continuation of three series already started. David Spriggs gave us an interesting series on twin parables in this issue, and in the next he continues this theme by looking at internal twin parables – parables within parables. Stephen Finamore also returns with part two of his four-part delve into Romans. And Isabelle Hamley returns from the May 2022 issue to bring us the second half of her reflections on Judges.

As we look towards Lent and Easter, we have three series that will speak to us during this period. Richard Martin will look at the Easter events themselves, while Tim Judson and Henry Wansbrough draw out key themes. Tim is a new contributor who will look at the important but often overlooked theme of lament, and Henry will explore the ideas of forgiveness and repentance.

We return to our regular gospel series alongside Andy Angel, who will be travelling with us through Matthew during 2023. Starting at chapter 15, he looks carefully at the events and themes in this gospel. We also have a fascinating two-week dive into Colossians from new contributor Johannes J. Knecht and an exciting fortnight of notes from Pauline Hoggarth on the lesser-known minor prophets: Habakkuk, Haggai, Nahum, Jonah.

We are also delighted to welcome Valerie Hobbs to *Guidelines*. An author and linguist, Valerie will explore the theme, 'Training our eyes for heaven', as she helps us negotiate 'this space of tension, fixed anxiously between earth and heaven'.

Finally, Phil Grasham returns with a series on traversing time and crossing cultures, thinking about how we engage with and interpret the Bible when the culture is so different – in time and space – to our own.

We hope you are looking forward to the 2023 issues. We certainly are, and hope they will bless you as you continue to meet God through his word.

What the Bible means to me:
Olivia Warburton

The decrees of the Lord are more precious than gold, than much pure gold; they are sweeter than honey, than honey from the honeycomb.

PSALM 19:10

We all know this, but do we live by it, day in, day out? I know I don't. Too busy not to pray? How about too busy not to seek God in scripture? It is, after all, possible to pray on the move; less easy with Bible reading.

But does it really matter? Here are ten things I've noticed start happening to me when Bible reading falls by the wayside. Perhaps they're true for you too.

1 Firstly, I develop **tunnel vision**. I see only my own priorities – which might well have started out as God's priorities once upon a time but somewhere along the way have become a little reworked – and find it harder to be open to God bringing in new things to my day. All I can see is what's already in front of me.

2 Next, I become **driven**. These priorities subtly take over. They become so important in my sight, I can't contemplate not delivering on them. They may be ever so worthy, but when – if – I stop to think about it, I'm not convinced God's necessarily as bothered about the progress of my to-do list as I am.

3 And then it all becomes rather **desperate**. My identity is wrapped up in what I'm trying to achieve. I worry about not getting the job done, or not getting it done well; about disappointing people or letting them down.

4 There's a constant niggle of **dissatisfaction** too, that things would be done better, or that somehow, nebulously, life would just be better, if only I had more time and energy.

5 Did I mention that I start to **detach**? No time for meaningful interactions or relationships when there's so much that needs doing.

6 **Dryness** follows. I'm thirsty, but not drinking the living water. Little spiritual refreshment, few moments of connection with God, a lack of

fresh, holy perspective on situations or challenges. And by the way, as an editor I read the Bible for a living. I have high levels of exposure to Bible content every single day. But engaging with it is a very different matter. I deceive myself if I think otherwise.

7   What then? Usually serious **tiredness**. I know that reading the Bible can restore my strength, but bizarrely it seems too much trouble even to open it.

8   **Demotivation** may follow, along with **doubt** that the task (I've) set before me is really worth doing after all, or that I'm the right person to do it.

9   Left unchecked, holding it all together may get too much and I begin to fray at the edges, or, worse, come apart at the seams. Relationships **deteriorate**, emotions are out of control and one thing after another starts going wrong.

10 Which is pretty **depressing**. If I get to this point, I'm feeling low and anxious and maybe it's even becoming obvious to other people that all is not well. Because it's amazing how good we are most of the time at keeping up appearances.

Does all this sound over the top? I don't think so. It's what happens when we move God from the centre, and by calling it out we can be clearer about the need for a remedy, and more inclined to seek it.

Psalm 19 continues: 'Who can discern their own errors? Forgive my hidden faults' (verse 12). And we can be encouraged by the confidence of the next words: 'Then I will be blameless, innocent of great transgression' (verse 13).

I am grateful that our loving, forgiving God speaks to us through the pages of the Bible – and in so many other ways – to remake us in his image daily.

Recommended reading

Join Sally Welch in BRF's Advent book for 2022, as she explores two questions: what is the Christmas story really about, and how do we share it?

Through each week of Advent, a different aspect of the Christmas story is examined: light, promise, mystery, love, peace and hope. Within each week, the days are focused on the ways in which the Christmas story is shared: prophecies, journeys, new life, signs, poems, stories and conversations. Each day offers a Bible passage, followed by a reflection, questions and a prayer. Suggestions for group study and creative prayer activities are also included.

The following is an edited extract taken from the first week of readings.

Mary and Elizabeth are two ordinary women in extraordinary situations. One of them has lived a long life and a good one. She has been faithful in her religious and domestic life, but although this has brought the reward of stability and love, the satisfaction of knowing she has done her duty to God, her husband and her community, she still lacks that most precious gift of all – a child, and she suffers for this. For her and her husband, the time of hope is past and she must live with her dearest longing unfulfilled. But then extraordinary things happens: her husband is struck dumb and she is with child. What a swirl of disbelief, of joy, of hardly-dared hoped-for happiness she must be living in! How many times a day must her feelings change – from excitement to anxiety and then once again to pure joy at her changed circumstances. Then in the sixth month of this emotional rollercoaster she has a visitor – her cousin Mary. Mary, another ordinary person, but young, very young. She is not yet married, but she is pregnant, and overwhelmed by this news has hurried to share it with her older, wiser cousin. An angel has visited her and told her she will be the God-bearer – and her life will never be the same again.

And as Mary hurries over the hills and plains to give and receive comfort and company, in her head is a song. It is not a song of fear or anxiety. It is not a song of self-concerned preoccupation about how changed her life has been. It is not the song of an oppressed people, suffering under the reign of their conquerors, forced to live under Roman occupation. It is not a song which will be sung to the mighty and the powerful. Mary sings a song of praise for her creator, the one who loves her and her people so much that he has come down to live among them, to show them how to live. Mary sings a song of thanksgiving for her life and for the life of the one she carries. Mary sings a song of prophecy, looking forward to a time when wrongs will be righted, when the good will triumph, the poor will suffer no more and mercy will flow down from the hills to flood the plains with righteousness.

Prior to Mary's visit, Elizabeth had shut herself away: 'After this, his wife Elizabeth became pregnant and remained in seclusion for five months. She said, "This is what the Lord did for me when he looked favourably on me and took away my public disgrace"' (Luke 1:24–25, ISV). She recognises that God has done a wonderful thing and perhaps she needs time to reflect on this and prepare for the birth. But Mary breaks in on her isolation, just as her song breaks into the perceived status quo of occupied Israel. Things will forever after be different. The news of God breaking into the world is broken between two women in a nondescript town in an occupied country. The established order is turned upside down. But this does not happen in one time or place. Mary speaks in the aorist tense, the past tense. She is acknowledging the action of God through the ages, the God who has been on the side of the oppressed and downtrodden since the time of their slavery in Egypt, the one who has been making and keeping promises since the time of Abraham. What has happened in the past will become the template for the future, and Mary is part of the path which leads towards the redemption of all people.

When we sing this song – whether it is a frozen few gathered in the chilly pews of a tiny rural church on a cold winter's evening, or whether the sound of the words drifts up into the golden rafters of a magnificent cathedral as hundreds of people join together in glorious praise – when we sing this song, we echo Mary's prayer of thanksgiving and rejoicing in the first stage of God's plan for his children. We celebrate all that has been achieved and look forward to all that will come, and we wait for the redemption of the world.

To order a copy of this book, please use the order form on page 151 or visit **brfonline.org.uk**.

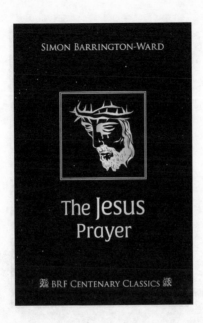

SIMON BARRINGTON-WARD

The Jesus Prayer

❀ BRF CENTENARY CLASSICS ❀

'Lord Jesus Christ, Son of God, have mercy on me.' This ancient prayer has been known and loved by generations of Christians for hundreds of years. It is a way of entering into the river of prayer which flows from the heart of God: the prayer of God himself, as Jesus continually prays for his people and for the world he loves. Simon Barrington-Ward teaches us how to use the Jesus Prayer as a devotional practice, and opens up the Bible passages that are crucial to understanding it.

The Jesus Prayer
Simon Barrington-Ward
978 1 80039 087 4 £14.99 hardback
brfonline.org.uk

RACHEL BOULDING

Companions
on the
Bethlehem Road

🎋 BRF CENTENARY CLASSICS 🎋

There are so many aspects of God's love for us and ours for him that are hard to grasp. While we can glimpse only part of the picture, it often seems that, in poetry, our deepest yearnings can come to the surface. As we travel the road to Christmas in the company of these great poets, we will find our minds enlarged and our hearts touched with something of the wonder and joy of this special season.

Companions on the Bethlehem Road
Rachel Boulding
978 1 80039 088 1 £14.99 hardback
brfonline.org.uk

To order

Online: **brfonline.org.uk**
Telephone: +44 (0)1865 319700
Mon–Fri 9.30–17.00

Delivery times within the UK are normally 15 working days. Prices are correct at the time of going to press but may change without prior notice.

Title	Price	Qty	Total
Sharing the Christmas Story	£8.99		
The BRF Book of 100 Prayers	£12.99		
The BRF Book of 365 Bible Reflections	£14.99		
The Jesus Prayer	£14.99		
Companions on the Bethlehem Road	£14.99		

POSTAGE AND PACKING CHARGES			
Order value	UK	Europe	Rest of world
Under £7.00	£2.00		
£7.00–£29.99	£3.00	Available on request	Available on request
£30.00 and over	FREE		

Total value of books	
Donation*	
Postage and packing	
Total for this order	

* Please complete and return the Gift Aid declaration on page 141.

Please complete in BLOCK CAPITALS

Title .... First name/initials .... Surname..

Address...

.... Postcode ....

Acc. No. .... Telephone ....

Email..

Method of payment

❑ Cheque (made payable to BRF) ❑ MasterCard / Visa

Card no. ☐☐☐☐ ☐☐☐☐ ☐☐☐☐ ☐☐☐☐ ☐☐☐☐ ☐☐☐

Expires end ☐☐ ☐☐ Security code ☐☐☐ Last 3 digits on the reverse of the card

We will use your personal data to process this order. From time to time we may send you information about the work of BRF. Please contact us if you wish to discuss your mailing preferences **brf.org.uk/privacy**

Please return this form to:

BRF, 15 The Chambers, Vineyard, Abingdon OX14 3FE | **enquiries@brf.org.uk**

For terms and cancellation information, please visit **brfonline.org.uk/terms**.

Bible Reading Fellowship is a charity (233280) and company limited by guarantee (301324), registered in England and Wales

Volunteering with BRF

At BRF we believe that volunteers have so much to contribute to our work and ministry as we support churches in their mission. We offer numerous opportunities, including the Local Church Champion role, whereby a volunteer shares the work of BRF with their local church.

Offering such a wealth of ministries for all ages, we are well placed to support churches in a way that is suitable for them and their context.

Our volunteers working with church leadership are able to make a difference to the lives of others.

The team includes people from a variety of ages, denominations and backgrounds, each with varying skills. Some have a particular BRF ministry of interest, while others are connected across all ministries.

The role is flexible to fit with each person's availability and varies in each setting. Some share information via their church notice sheet or have contact with specific individuals such as children's or youth workers or those working with older people. Others have contacts in their Churches Together network or denominational structures. Being well supported by BRF offers an opportunity to feel connected as well as getting to know others in a similar role.

Angela in Wiltshire volunteered, with the encouragement of her rector, to encourage individuals and groups to get closer to God through regular study by highlighting the various BRF resources and updates in the parish newsletter.

Catriona Foster, a volunteer, shares:

I would sum up my volunteering with BRF as a rewarding and inspiring privilege. Not only is volunteering rewarding and enjoyable but recent research has shown that well-being is significantly improved when people are meeting and helping others and feel valued.

As volunteer Martyn Payne so helpfully expresses:

It is when we reach out to help others that we are most helped – this is the surprising equation of giving and receiving that lies at the heart of our faith in God.

If you or someone you know would be interested in joining the team, do contact **jane.butcher@brf.org.uk**.

Enabling all ages to grow in faith

At BRF, we long for people of all ages to grow in faith and understanding of the Bible. That's what all our work as a charity is about.

- Our **Living Faith** range of resources helps Christians go deeper in their understanding of scripture, in prayer and in their walk with God. Our conferences and events bring people together to share this journey, while our Holy Habits initiative helps whole congregations grow together as disciples of Jesus, living out and sharing their faith.

- We also want to make it easier for local churches to engage effectively in ministry and mission – by helping them bring new families into a growing relationship with God through **Messy Church** or by supporting churches as they nurture the spiritual life of older people through **Anna Chaplaincy**.

- Our **Parenting for Faith** team coaches parents and others to raise God-connected children and teens, and enables churches to fully support them.

Do you share our vision?

Though a significant proportion of BRF's funding is generated through our charitable activities, we are dependent on the generous support of individuals, churches and charitable trusts.

If you share our vision, would you help us to enable even more people of all ages to grow in faith? Your prayers and financial support are vital for the work that we do. You could:

- Support BRF's ministry with a regular donation;
- Support us with a one-off gift;
- Consider leaving a gift to BRF in your will (see page 154);
- Encourage your church to support BRF as part of your church's giving to home mission – perhaps focusing on a specific ministry or programme;
- Most important of all, support BRF with your prayers.

Donate at **brf.org.uk/donate** or use the form on pages 141–42.

Planning for the future

For I know the plans I have for you, declares the Lord, plans for welfare and not for evil, to give you a future and a hope.
JEREMIAH 29:11 (ESV)

Change is inevitable, and in recent years the idea of the unexpected has become so familiar one might even say that it is expected! In times of turmoil and unpredictability, it is a comfort and a blessing to hold these words dear. Where our plans may seem like an utter mess, God has a plan for us, and one that promises hope.

Jeremiah's words were written to Jewish people who had been forced by their enemies to settle in a foreign country. They were written to people who may have desired a quick fix, a promise of immediate safety and security. Instead, God instead promises that he has a plan, that he will give them a future and a hope.

Making plans for the long term can be intimidating, especially when thinking about the future and providing for our loved ones. But we can make those plans in the knowledge that God knows what lies ahead and is here for us in the present to show us into a hopeful future.

One important way to plan for the future is to make a will. Many people find this to be an anxious or complicated process, but it does not need to be. At BRF, we are reliant on fundraising activities, donations and gifts in wills to enable us to carry out our work. We are hugely grateful to everyone who remembers BRF in their will or who makes a donation in memory of a loved one.

After you have made provision for your family, friends and church, maybe you would kindly consider a gift of 1% in your will to help BRF. We always recommend visiting a solicitor to ensure that your will accurately represents your wishes. All you will need to take to your solicitor is our registered charity number, which is 233280.

If you would like any more information on making a gift to BRF in your will please do get in touch with our fundraising team on **01235 462305** or via **giving@brf.org.uk**.

We thank you for your support and your prayers.

The BRF fundraising team

Please note our new subscription rates, current until 30 April 2023:

Individual subscriptions
covering 3 issues for under 5 copies, payable in advance
(including postage & packing):

	UK	Europe	Rest of world
Guidelines 1-year subscription	£18.30	£26.25	£30.15
Guidelines 3-year subscription (9 issues)	£53.55	N/A	N/A

Group subscriptions
covering 3 issues for 5 copies or more, sent to one UK address (post free):

Guidelines 1-year subscription	£14.55 per set of 3 issues p.a.

Please note that the annual billing period for group subscriptions runs from 1 May to 30 April.

Overseas group subscription rates
Available on request. Please email **enquiries@brf.org.uk**.

Copies may also be obtained from Christian bookshops:

Guidelines	£4.85 per copy

All our Bible reading notes can be ordered online
by visiting **brfonline.org.uk/subscriptions**

GUIDELINES

Guidelines is also available as
an app for Android, iPhone and iPad
brfonline.org.uk/apps

GUIDELINES INDIVIDUAL SUBSCRIPTION FORM

> All our Bible reading notes can be ordered online by visiting
> **brfonline.org.uk/subscriptions**

Title _____ First name/initials _____ Surname _____

Address _____

_____ Postcode _____

Telephone _____ Email _____

Please send *Guidelines* beginning with the January 2023 / May 2023 /
September 2023 issue (*delete as appropriate*):

(*please tick box*)	UK	Europe	Rest of world
Guidelines 1-year subscription	☐ £18.30	☐ £26.25	☐ £30.15
Guidelines 3-year subscription	☐ £53.55	N/A	N/A

Optional donation to support the work of BRF £ _____

Total enclosed £ _____ (cheques should be made payable to 'BRF')

Please complete and return the Gift Aid declaration on page 141 to make your
donation even more valuable to us.

Please charge my MasterCard / Visa with £ _____

Card no. ☐☐☐☐ ☐☐☐☐ ☐☐☐☐ ☐☐☐☐

Expires end ☐☐ M M ☐☐ Y Y   Security code ☐☐☐   Last 3 digits on the reverse of the card

To set up a Direct Debit, please complete the Direct Debit instruction on page 159.

Please return this form to:
BRF, 15 The Chambers, Vineyard, Abingdon OX14 3FE

For terms and cancellation information, please visit **brfonline.org.uk/terms**.

Bible Reading Fellowship is a charity (233280) and company limited by guarantee (301324),
registered in England and Wales

GL0322

GUIDELINES GIFT SUBSCRIPTION FORM

☐ I would like to give a gift subscription (please provide both names and addresses):

Title .... First name/initials .... Surname ....

Address ....

.... Postcode ....

Telephone .... Email ....

Gift subscription name ....

Gift subscription address ....

.... Postcode ....

Gift message (20 words max. or include your own gift card):

....

....

Please send *Guidelines* beginning with the January 2023 / May 2023 / September 2023 issue *(delete as appropriate)*:

(please tick box)	UK	Europe	Rest of world
Guidelines 1-year subscription	☐ £18.30	☐ £26.25	☐ £30.15
Guidelines 3-year subscription	☐ £53.55	N/A	N/A

Optional donation to support the work of BRF £ ....

Total enclosed £ .... (cheques should be made payable to 'BRF')

Please complete and return the Gift Aid declaration on page 141 to make your donation even more valuable to us.

Please charge my MasterCard / Visa with £ ....

Card no. ☐☐☐☐ ☐☐☐☐ ☐☐☐☐ ☐☐☐☐

Expires end [M][M] [Y][Y] Security code ☐☐☐ Last 3 digits on the reverse of the card

To set up a Direct Debit, please complete the Direct Debit instruction on page 159.

Please return this form to:
BRF, 15 The Chambers, Vineyard, Abingdon OX14 3FE

For terms and cancellation information, please **visit brfonline.org.uk/terms**.

Bible Reading Fellowship is a charity (233280) and company limited by guarantee (301324), registered in England and Wales

DIRECT DEBIT PAYMENT

You can pay for your annual subscription to our Bible reading notes using Direct Debit. You need only give your bank details once, and the payment is made automatically every year until you cancel it. If you would like to pay by Direct Debit, please use the form opposite, entering your BRF account number under 'Reference number'.

You are fully covered by the Direct Debit Guarantee:

The Direct Debit Guarantee

- This Guarantee is offered by all banks and building societies that accept instructions to pay Direct Debits.
- If there are any changes to the amount, date or frequency of your Direct Debit, Bible Reading Fellowship will notify you 10 working days in advance of your account being debited or as otherwise agreed. If you request Bible Reading Fellowship to collect a payment, confirmation of the amount and date will be given to you at the time of the request.
- If an error is made in the payment of your Direct Debit, by Bible Reading Fellowship or your bank or building society, you are entitled to a full and immediate refund of the amount paid from your bank or building society.
- If you receive a refund you are not entitled to, you must pay it back when Bible Reading Fellowship asks you to.
- You can cancel a Direct Debit at any time by simply contacting your bank or building society. Written confirmation may be required. Please also notify us.

Instruction to your bank or building society to pay by Direct Debit

Please fill in the whole form using a ballpoint pen and return with order form to:
BRF, 15 The Chambers, Vineyard, Abingdon OX14 3FE

Service User Number: | 5 | 5 | 8 | 2 | 2 | 9 |

Name and full postal address of your bank or building society

To: The Manager	Bank/Building Society
Address	
	Postcode

Name(s) of account holder(s)

Branch sort code

| | | – | | | – | | | |

Bank/Building Society account number

| | | | | | | | | |

Reference number

| | | | | | | | |

Instruction to your Bank/Building Society
Please pay Bible Reading Fellowship Direct Debits from the account detailed
in this instruction, subject to the safeguards assured by the Direct Debit Guarantee.
I understand that this instruction may remain with Bible Reading Fellowship
and, if so, details will be passed electronically to my bank/building society.

Signature(s)

Banks and Building Societies may not accept Direct Debit instructions for some
types of account.